SAGGISTICA 29

TRANSLATING FOR (AND FROM) THE ITALIAN SCREEN
DUBBING AND SUBTITLES

TRANSLATING FOR (AND FROM) THE ITALIAN SCREEN
DUBBING AND SUBTITLES

Edited by
Philip Balma
Giovanni Spani

BORDIGHERA PRESS

Library of Congress Control Number: 2019937312

COVER IMAGE: *Tokyo Eye*
by Claudio Bettio

Printed in the United States.

Published by
BORDIGHERA PRESS
John D. Calandra Italian American Institute
25 West 43rd Street, 17th Floor
New York, NY 10036

SAGGISTICA 29
ISBN 978-1-59954-141-9

TABLE OF CONTENTS

PREFACE

In 20th century Italy, as is still the case to this day, the film and television industries found themselves in constant competition with a wealth of Anglophone (and mostly American) foreign products that are frequently projected in theaters and/or broadcast on TV. In the Italian context and in a select number of other countries all of these products undergo the process of dubbing before they are distributed and screened. In the United States, on the other hand, foreign films are typically subtitled in English without the use of a translated voice track.

Although he passed away in 2001, the most iconic (and still recognizable) dubber and voice actor in Italian history was certainly Ferruccio Amendola. In fact, even if this was not done by design, his voice can be heard in the Italophone version of multiple features referenced in this volume. He was not simply iconic because of his significant talent and the ubiquitous presence of his voice in major international box office hits. His voice became the filter, if you will, for some of the best-known cinematic characters of his century—it became synonymous with the most heroic protagonists, or sometimes the most notorious villains—and it remains easily identifiable for a large majority of Italians born before the turn of the millennium. Imagine being called upon to have your name and (especially) your speech patterns indelibly associated with entire filmic franchises, such as the *Rambo* and *Rocky* movies starring Sylvester Stallone, but also being hired to voice Al Capone in *The Untouchables* and Tony Montana in De Palma's remake of *Scarface*. Depending on the specific film and its cast, Amendola also had the opportunity to dub an incredible array of internationally-acclaimed actors. There are so many of them worth mentioning that it would be impossible to acknowledge all of them in the span of this short preface. Suffice it to say that his work has allowed him to dub the likes of Dustin Hoffman, Peter Falk, James Woods, Harvey Keitel, Clint Eastwood, Peter Fonda, Richard Pryor, Steve Martin and many other greats, including Edward G. Robinson on at least one occasion. Perhaps more than any other dubbing artist, Amendola shaped the way in which American culture was transmitted to Italian audiences during his time. His professionalism and work ethic are both reflected in his considerable successes as well as the impact he has had in his chosen profession.

The responsibility Ferruccio Amendola and his colleagues share(d) in rendering American/Anglophone voice tracks for Italian film and TV viewers is humongous. Italy's dubbing industry is as prolific as it is successful and (usually) faithful to the source material in translation. When someone fell short and failed to achieve this standard, regardless of the reasons why, linguistic and cultural misreadings and misunderstandings took place which were then distributed to millions of viewers. The same could be said, unfortunately, for the countless occasions in which utterances in the Italian language were mistranslated (in a system of subtitles) for Anglophone audiences. Intended for those readers whose interests include Cinema and Television as well as Italian culture and Translation Studies, this book represents an important step in addressing unique forms of trans-national, cross-cultural exchanges that take place every single day, anywhere films and television shows can be viewed. This is a responsibility that the authors of this study have embraced with enthusiasm and caution alike, in the hopes that other scholars might continue in their footsteps.

Philip Balma
University of Connecticut

Giovanni Spani
College of the Holy Cross

TRANSLATING FOR (AND FROM) THE ITALIAN SCREEN
DUBBING AND SUBTITLES

Dubbing America and Subtitling Italy
A Short Introduction

From the incomplete system of subtitles that accompanied the first American screenings of Rossellini's *Rome Open City* to the linguistic acrobatics that characterized the Italian dubbing of the Detroit-based movie *8 Mile* (starring international rap star Eminem), the Italian and American film industries have almost always interacted through a process of textual or verbal translation. With the exception of the province of Quebec, in the North American continent foreign films are typically subtitled. In France, Italy, Germany, and Spain (known as the FIGS group), most foreign films undergo the process of dubbing. In the 1950s these countries introduced measures to control and lessen the impact of American films in their markets, including domestic production quotas and special import taxes. The systematic use of dubbing in Italy dates back to the 1930s in Rome, Milan, and Turin. A fascist ban on foreign languages made it obligatory to dub foreign movies into Italian in 1933, creating a thriving dubbing industry for movies, documentaries, and cartoons. Although nowadays in larger Italian cities some foreign films are screened both in Italian and in their original version, almost all American movies are still dubbed in Italian to this day, and the same can be said for a great majority of American TV shows.

It's not so surprising, then, that the late comedic actor Alberto Sordi began his career by dubbing Oliver Hardy, producing a humorous Anglo-Italian hybrid that has achieved an iconic status in popular Italian culture. Perhaps one of the most talented and best-known Italian dubbing artists was Ferruccio Amendola, who lent his voice to big American actors like DeNiro, Pacino, Hoffman and Stallone. Another noteworthy figure is Oreste Lionello, the actor who became the Italian voice for Woody Allen and also dubbed a number of other international stars over the years, including Peter Sellers and Charlie Chaplin.

A very small percentage of Italian films have actually been dubbed into English for Anglophone audiences. A version of Ettore Scola's award-winning *Una giornata particolare* (A Special Day, 1977) is available for purchase with a language track that includes the real voices of Sophia Loren and Marcello Mastroianni reciting their lines in English, showing an enviable command of the language in fact, with the understandable exception of a recognizable Italian accent. This feature, for which Mastroianni received an Oscar Nomination in the coveted category of 'Best Actor in a Leading Role,' is however mostly unknown to the average American/Anglophone filmgoer. The same cannot be said, however, for Roberto Benigni's Holocaust film *La vita è bella* (Life is Beautiful, 1997), which won our director-protagonist Benigni the same Oscar that Mastroianni *could* have won. Originally released in Italian with subtitles in American theatres, after its highly visible success at the Academy Awards in 1999 (bringing home a total of three statues including Best Foreign Language Film), *Life is Beautiful* was re-released in movie theatres in the United States with an English language track, in an effort to further boost its popularity and box office success in the Anglophone world. In other words, even when the American film industry finds that an Italian motion picture warrants special attention and may be particularly profitable, aside from ensuring it is screened in many theatres, sold on pay-per-view and purchased or rented on

DVD, said work is *very rarely* re-released in English in cinemas. Metaphorically speaking, and setting aside the complex capitalistic implications of this discourse, it's the 'highest honor' that is only occasionally granted to a foreign feature film in the United States.

In Europe, and especially in Western Europe, American films and television programs are routinely dubbed for mass distribution and broadcast. This volume examines the process of linguistic and socio-cultural translation that takes place when films are dubbed or subtitled, endeavoring to explore the complex interplay of both deliberate and accidental meanings that are constructed when a film reaches a broader audience through the intervention of a translator. Though our scope is confined to the context of works that are imported or exported to and from Italy, this study engages multiple genres (comedy, action, Sci-Fi, etc.) and the efforts that made it possible to screen specific filmic products in different continents and countries, as well as the important and innovative ways in which dubbed films and television shows can be used in the foreign language classroom. Inevitably, in this line of inquiry one must contend with the creative (and, at times, ineffective) strategies employed in rendering specific Anglo-American or Italian cultural elements in translation. It's impossible, for example, not to mention the unique case of *La tata*, the Italian-dubbed version of the popular television sit-com *The Nanny*. The Italophone dubbers made a complex and unusual choice in this case when they decided to use the process of linguistic filtration to 'excise' the protagonist's Jewish identity, transforming her instead into an Italian-American woman who has little to no connection to the Jewish community in the States. Although there certainly are many examples of egregiously flawed translations of cinematic or televised works that one might focus on in order to express the urgency (and the breadth) of the field of knowledge being tackled in these pages, *La tata/The Nanny* is not one of those cases. It is not 'flawed;' but rather, it reflects a strong cultural and ethno-religious imbalance between the schemata of the average consumer of American television products *in* America when compared to a typical Italian TV viewer in the 20th and 21st centuries. Italian Jews consist of a fraction of 1% of the population, and are often absent or misrepresented in modern Italian media, but the real obstacles faced by *La tata*'s dubbing team were linguistic as well as cultural in nature. *The Nanny*'s original version included the usage of a number of terms and references to ritualistic and cultural notions that are specific to Jewish life. These elements are familiar enough to the average American viewer, and the show's success is a confirmation of this fact. *La tata*, instead, in its Italianized and Italophone version, met the cultural expectations (and entertainment needs) of its intended audience, and it did so through a rather intricate and unusual experiment. This is but one of hundreds (if not thousands) of instances in which fictional films, documentaries, or TV shows are mistranslated by design. Other examples include the works of important and socially engaged Italian directors such as Nanni Moretti or the late Pier Paolo Pasolini, whose efforts may have suffered from censorship "after the fact," so to speak, given that some of the original (and politically sensitive) content of one of his films was 'modified' for foreign audiences through a system of inaccurate Anglophone subtitles.

One needn't travel abroad, however, to find evidence of how Italian (or dialectal) language has weighed heavily on the impact and reception of cinematic works, including award-winning American blockbuster films, such as Coppola's *The Godfather*, adapted from Mario Puzo's homonymous best-selling novel. On this side of the Atlantic Ocean, occasional uses of Italian or expressions and exchanges in Italian dialect in a project filmed in English might end up grossly mistranslated in the subtitles, and the amount of money spent making the film could possibly have no quantifiable connection to the quality of these translations, even in the case of a prestigious and potentially award-worthy motion picture. It's futile to speculate at length as to how or why these things happen: in a film that boasts one of the most star-studded casts in 20th century Hollywood history, a short but heated argument in Italian can get mangled to the point where the only connection between what the characters are saying (or screaming) and the subtitles is the notion that our interlocutors are clearly very upset. Levinson's 1996 stunning crime drama *Sleepers*, starring the likes of Brad Pitt, Dustin Hoffman, Robert DeNiro, Minnie Driver, Kevin Bacon, and Italy's own Vittorio Gassman is unfortunately one of these films. Based on Lorenzo Carcaterra's 1995 novel by the same name, this picture offers a significant amount of character development of the protagonist "Shakes," including his youth and difficult adolescence. Faced with the inevitable prospect of ending up in a juvenile detention facility, Shakes informs his father who flies off the handle, yelling and throwing objects around, shattering them into pieces. Frightened and in tears, Shakes' mother (who speaks Italian fluently but struggles in English) implores her husband to stop by shouting "Basta!" at him. In the same exact moment, Shakes asks her to make him calm down ("Ma', fallo calmare!"). This incredibly brief and highly tense exchange is the only moment in the film when Italian is used, yet the "official" subtitles for this film, projected on the big screen in theatres and (now) available on "Region 1" DVD copies, miss the mark so badly that it's beyond redemption. English words that vaguely sound like the ones used in Italian appeared in the subtitles, so a terrified immigrant mother, who may very well fear her own safety and her child's to be at risk (given how furious her spouse his), shouts the insult "Bastard!" at him instead of telling him to stop. To make matters worse, in lieu of begging his mom to calm down his father, in the subtitles Shakes verbally assaults him as well, disrespectfully telling him to "Fucking calm down!" – as if this would help contain the man's anger.

Given the hegemonic status enjoyed worldwide by American products (cultural or otherwise), it's important to consider that even after the dubbing process Hollywood productions make up a significant chunk of the films available in Italian film theatres (and in Europe in general). Since Italians started dubbing foreign films back in the 1930s, the more than 8 decades of dubbed foreign films that have made their way into the annals of Italian film history constitute a gargantuan amount of fertile ground for academic inquiry. It would be sufficient, in fact, to analyze how American film titles have been translated in Italy to discern an important initial set of patterns that govern these international renditions of filmic works and, of course, the reasons behind some of their successes, mistakes, pitfalls, and moments of both intentional and accidental genius.

Let us restrict our focus to a handful of popular films from the late 20th century to clarify this point. Weintraub's 1984 smash hit *The Karate Kid*, which put young Ralph Macchio on the map, was titled *Per vincere domani*. This can be translated as "To Win Tomorrow," so a film that centers around a karate tournament in this case gave away the protagonist's victorious ending in the second word of the title. Since *The Karate Kid* eventually became a franchise and multiple sequels were shot, the subsequent movies in this series used/included the English title (for example: *Karate Kid II, la storia continua* was released in Italy in 1986).

Some choices might seem fairly obvious and practical given the phonetic difficulties encountered by many Italians in pronouncing specific English words and names. In the Italian version of *The Cosby Show*, for this reason, the Huxtable family was re-named *I Robinson* (The Robinsons), which became the new title of the program. One can assume that the difficulty in pronouncing a specific word was also a key reason why Darabont's *The Shawshank Redemption* (1994) became *Le ali della libertà* (The Wings of Freedom).

Some translations, on the other hand, may strike an English-speaking viewer as both random and potentially unnecessary. If the titles *Star Wars* (Guerre Stellari) and *Spaceballs* (Balle Spaziali) were both successfully rendered, and the more challenging TV show title *Knight Rider* was intelligently called *Supercar*, then why did *Family Ties* starring Michael J. Fox have to be titled *Casa Keaton* (The Keaton Home), and why could they not find a better title for the show *Growing Pains* than *Genitori in blue jeans* (Parents in blue jeans)? The cartoon characters known as *The Smurfs* are named *Puffi* in Italian, and they were created (and differently named) by a Belgian artist, so neither version is technically ideal, yet the names work, they are creative solutions that satisfy a need by making use of a poetic license. Furthermore, given that Italian high schools have historically made use of a bell to signal the beginning and the end of specific class periods to students and teachers, there truly is no reason why the popular show *Saved By The Bell* could not have been called something resembling "salvato dalla campanella" instead of *Bayside School*. In short, examples of inaccurately translated titles abound on TV and the silver screen and, in some cases, they can significantly contribute to a process that alters or compromises how filmic works are received by viewers and marketed through advertisement. Scholars of Film Studies who are multilingual, and especially those with experience in the field of Translation Studies, share a common responsibility to analyze, interpret, and – if needed – to rectify those failed efforts that run the risk of misleading their audience or misrepresenting the motion picture or TV program in question, yet the real reason why this volume came to be is a different one. Dubbing and subtitles are a reality (and the standard) in today's film and television industry, and this fact is not going to change anytime soon. These practices, which most often highlight the skill, ingenuity and creativity of professional dubbing teams, also constitute important vehicles for the transmission and exportation of national cultures and their artistic products. As such, they are necessary to ensure that at least an important amount of "passive" cultural exchanges can take place, that more viewers are able to explore different peoples, countries and distant environments in cinemas or in the comfort of their homes.

In the 1930s, when Italian journalist Leo Longanesi claimed that films had replaced novels as the new models for the youth, he was making an observation *and* a prediction of sorts, given that his statement is more accurate today than it was eight decades ago. In the United States, for example, one could ask hundreds of college-age students if they have seen more movies or read more books in their lifetime, and a minimum of 90% of them would admit to having seen more films. In light of the ease with which American culture and values are distributed, screened, and broadcast worldwide on a mass scale, the way these notions are in turn communicated to foreign audiences is not without consequences or far-reaching ramifications. The same must be said, of course, for all films and TV shows when they are examined in an international, multilingual context. In fact, in bringing this short essay to its conclusion it's worth considering one additional piece of anecdotal evidence. The aforementioned show *Saved by the Bell* appeared on American screens from 1989 to 1993, but it was only dubbed in Italian and broadcast (as *Bayside School*) on the channel *Italia 1* after its conclusion. In France, on the other hand, this program was dubbed and broadcast on *Antenne 2* almost immediately, so when the show appeared on TV as *Sauvés par le gong* (lit: *Saved by the Bell*), its success roughly coincided with the same period of time in which its 'American counterpart' was gaining much popularity among young American viewers.

Long before digital televisions and High-Definition flat-screen TVs existed, anyone possessing a regular ("rabbit ears") antenna and a functioning TV set could watch the French channel *Antenne 2* in Italy at any time. For the span of four years (1989-1993), any young ex-pats based in Italy who were fans of the show could hence choose between never seeing it at all or watching it in another romance language. Regardless of one's relative level of comprehension of French, a number of American cultural elements (and stereotypes) were easily recognizable, such as the characters' clothing, hair styles, musical tastes, and several notions related to dating and romantic relationships among high school students. What went missing, or rather, 'unheard' in this unique trans-lingual viewing experience isn't just necessary to clarify the major events of the plot. Even when the underlying message of an individual episode is easy enough to grasp from beyond the language barrier, only a French speaker could truly come to understand what these characters mean to each other, the depth of their bonds, as well as the tone and subtleties of their specific utterances, since not all gags or jokes were accompanied by a laugh-track to 'guide' viewers in their appreciation of the comedic value of the show. In other words, the most important information about these young characters was all placed in the hands of dubbers: that which makes them human, and that which distinguishes them as unique human beings.

Philip Balma
Giovanni Spani
Worcester, Massachusetts

This book is dedicated to the memory of our former professor, one of the most prolific American scholars of Italian Cinema. Peter Bondanella (1943-2017), was Distinguished Professor Emeritus of Italian, Comparative Literature, and Film Studies at Indiana University, Bloomington.

Versioning Audiovisual Humor
The Rendition of Comedic Language In Italian

Luca Barattoni

> Dubbing undermines the believability of whatever reality
> the filmic representation can offer, of the other and their
> social and cultural world: it creates a fictitious domestici-
> ty that is perceived by the spectator as incongruous and
> reduces the film to disposable spectacle, vitiating its em-
> pathic valence.
>
> (Sisto 2014: 9)

1. TRANSLATION THEORY AND THE PROBLEM OF HUMOR

Several models of specialized audiovisual translation ac-
counting for the pragmatic, communicative and semiotic di-
mensions of the interrelation between sound, image and text
have been advanced. Hatim and Mason (1990) gestured toward the act of translation as the response to a communicative discourse in which the translator operates as a negotiator
and problem-solver in a social framework. Venuti ventured
on a genealogical journey detailing the history of translation
practices to propose a new epistemological approach based
on "an aesthetic of discontinuity" (1995: 306), one always de-
claring its honesty regarding the tactics adopted to navigate
between different cultures and offset their unbalances. A
pragmatic approach was that of Zabalbeascoa (1996), who put
forward a functionalist model based on priority scales whereby the balance achieved among the many variables at work in
the translation would be crucial to surrogate the cultural lore
of the source material. Agost Canós (1999) further expanded

the notion of the translator as decision-maker, establishing a hierarchy of audiovisual genres and assessing the work of the translator as mediation among the configuring elements — factual context, technical and professional sphere — colliding during the translation process. An influential articulation advanced by Toury (1995) focused specifically on the cultural divides between texts and introduced the "descriptive" trope in Translation Studies in order to probe the broad, deep network of relations involved in the act of translating. The descriptive method emphasized the constrained nature of the cultural recodification of language and inscribed the translation process into always reconstituting dynamic norms, which "account for the relationships that exist between the rules of the abstract and modeling society and the idiosyncrasies of each translator" (Díaz Cintas 2004: 25).

Other theoretical avenues diagnosed the added difficulties in translating humor, assessing the appropriateness of replacements and substitutes in compensatory strategies, as well as the degree of creative reworking and refitting of elements from the original script. For instance, Delabastita operated from a descriptive framework and, after browsing the existing literature on the adaptation of jokes and puns, invoked "the adoption of a historical and norm-governed concept of both translation and wordplay" (1994: 241). Guido (2012) shrewdly bridged the gap between performance and authorship by advocating a cognitive-experientialist model of translation whereby the dubber, by inhabiting the physical space of the action on screen and entering into a new level of participation, will in turn holistically embody all the skills — linguistic, translating, acting, directing — necessary for a successful adaptation. Iaia's Interactive Model, assessing the "interaction between the source-text analysis and the creative contribution to T[arget]T[ext]s" (2015: 56) and echoing Jakobson's concept of intersemiotic transmutation as an act of awareness and acceptance, proves to be a powerful tool to determine the successful or failed transfer of the pragmatic coefficient between Source and Target Text. By taking into account "the integration between the cognitive, socio-cultural and linguistic features that interact in [humorous discourse]'s construction and interpretation" (2015: 59), Iaia disciplines the relationship between translators and source material, appraising the degree of reciprocal cooperation between audience and target text.

2. ITALY AND DUBBING:
POLITICAL CALCULUS DISGUISED AS BASIC NECESSITY

One aspect stands out when looking at the history of dubbing in Italy: Even before Fascism, the practice of post-synchronization of a different soundtrack is irredeemably intertwined with the exercise — if not with the very introduction — of censorship. The royal decree issued by Italy's prime minister, Giovanni Giolitti, on May 31, 1914, allowed for the presence of foreign languages in films as long as translations in Italian were also offered; however, the double version became immediately too expensive to provide and, as a result, foreign films were turned into rigidly monolingual artifacts. With the advent of sound in cinema, especially in the early 1930–1934 stage, the royal decree-law no. 5 of October 1933, prohibiting that dubbing be carried out abroad, seemed a natural expansion of the legislation intended to centralize and state-regulate every aspect of the censoring and control process. Another factor remained constant in the equation: right after its introduction "il principale mezzo di unificazione linguistica nazionale continua a essere l'audiovisivo" ("the main means of national linguistic unification continues to be audiovisual") (Paolinelli and Di Fortunato 2005: 8). The intention of domestic dubbing was to neutralize every foreign language into an artificial, wooden Italian—to homogenize dialects and create a regime-sanctioned Italian during Fascism, to alphabetize the population and attract audiences after the end of WWII.

No serious threat seems to jeopardize the practice today, with the dubbers well entrenched as a lobby and the audience resigned to the same voices covering actors and actresses speaking in different languages, with the occasional bravura pieces improving a film or two. In fact, the opposition has always seemed isolated and sporadic. Among the most authoritative and critical voices, one may mention Michelangelo Antonioni lamenting the estranging effect of dubbing in a series of articles published in the 1940s and American film specialists Guido Fink and Franco La Polla, in a roundtable with dubbing professionals Oreste Lionello and Gianni Galassi, noting the additional erasure and lack that dubbing entails as opposed to subtitling. However, if the final result is "the conventional use of a formal register and standard accents (a Tuscan-Roman variant)" as well as "the inability of the re-voiced Italian to substitute many colloquial and expressive features" (Mereu Keating 2012: 118), then a serious debate should be opened about which materials and which professionals should integrate with subtitling to preserve the integrity of the original artifact. It is hard not to agree with Sergio Raffaelli when he writes about the lingering effects of the Fascist legislation ("menomazioni non ancora sanate" ["impairments not yet remedied"] 2004: 67), preventing Italian audiences from comprehending the meanings contained in the original soundtracks.

3. MONTY PYTHON AND STEPHEN CHOW:
FROM CULTURAL DIFFERENCE TO CULTURAL REMOVE

> L'industria cinematografica italiana detiene un primato mondia-
> le che copre l'intera storia del sonoro e che consiste nell'applica-
> zione sistematica e indiscriminata del doppiaggio a tutti i film di
> produzione straniera, senza distinzione d'idioma, di paese, di
> genere, di metraggio (Raffaelli 2004: 63).
> [The Italian film industry holds a world record that covers the
> entire history of sound and consists of the systematic and indis-
> criminate application of dubbing to all films of foreign produc-
> tion, without distinction of language, country, genre, and footage].

With the advent of the globalized/globalizing platform disengaged from recognizable national and regional markers and the dilution of cultural specificities, dubbing becomes easier. The only exceptions to the inflexible totality Raffaelli describes are limited to specialized art house theaters and screenings for the international community. Because "dubbing reinforces, through a heightened illusionary translation process (going beyond lip sync), a sense of national identity and national belonging" (Ferrari 2006: 125), it is tempting to argue that such forays into versioning practices entailing not so subtle rewriting and brutal contortions of cues, references, and behaviors from the original script are met with resigned acceptance by Italian audiences. Even though "[m]ost Italians appear to be more tolerant than most Americans to visual dischrony, including lip dischrony and gesture and facial expression dischrony" (Gambier 2003: 173) there have been cases of openly Frankensteinian experiments on the filmic body. In other words, the taming strategies deployed to domesticate the *perceived* asperities in the original audiovisual product involve not only the neutralization of the cultural otherness but in some peculiarly infamous cases also lead to a thorough reconfiguration of the source material according to paradigms already experienced by the target audience.

Compensation is carried out through less culture-specific solutions that negate the breadth of the original version, and *Monty Python and the Holy Grail* (hereafter, *MPHG*; directed in 1975 by Terry Gilliam and Terry Jones) represents the point of no return of such an approach. For the analysis of this film, the Peircean model put forward by Adab (2006) seems particularly appropriate for its capacity to probe the damages caused by the erasure of interpretants after the dubbing process. Applying a strategy of reduction and neutralization of original references, the dubbers intervene in the "culturally acquired skills and recognition of the underlying structures involved" (Adab 2006: 188) and thereby nullify the interactive partnership between the film and its audience. Emerging from a world cinema era rich with parodic treatments, *MPHG* goes beyond a merely reactive approach lampooning the Hollywood treatment of medieval deeds and avoids with great care being pinned down to a specific genre:

> *Monty Python and the Holy Grail* is an artifact informed by the history of film and filmmaking, reflexive enough to acknowledge its pastiche nature as a shifting, postmodern construct, but aware, also, that it is a paeanic elegy to a dimming and diminished Great Britain (Larsen 2015: xii).

The emphasis on simultaneity of different historical planes does not subtract from the ethical discourse, though, making the film rather a modernist artifact where the pastiche technique is conducive to the annulment of chronological time. Reconstructing the Pythons' interest in Pasolini, Antonioni, Visconti and Bergman among others, Larsen ascribes *MPHG*—via David Bordwell's characterization of art house filmmaking—to a subcategory of art cinema parodying art cinema. Key elements of high modernist cinema are the fruit-less wandering, the "back to square one" ontological demise of the protagonists, the casual appearance and disappearance of purposes and goals that cannot be attained. The Pythons' subversive approach to the pomp and circumstance of official historiography is in full force, whereby "every presented real-ity can be undercut, reinformed and re-formed, leaving no stable narrative ground" (Larsen 2015: 344). In fact, one may stipulate a Deleuzian foray into sensory-motor breakdown territory, as in the scene where Lancelot runs and runs and runs only to be farther and farther from reaching an entry point. Similarly, the destruction of logical joints is accom-plished in the "realized metaphors" of the abuse and killing of the characters in the transition scenes.

The Italian dubbing transcends a mere erasure of the cul-tural significance and aims at a complete transformation of the artifact, repackaging *MPHG* into a hybrid showcase of en-tertainers, sport commentators and dubbing professionals mostly resorting to one of the cheapest means to elicit a re-sponse from the Italian audience: dialectal sterotypicality. With that approach, all the translation strategies listed by Gambier—"language and register variation, strategies of re-duction, omission, neutralization and expansion" (2003: 183) —are conveniently bundled together to ensure a complete bastardization of the humor via a soundtrack of conventional regional frequencies. As a result, the final product is a disso-nant and unbalanced act. The Arthurian epic seamlessly shifts to a quixotic pattern of dismissal and failure; the *MPHG* script moves fluidly from episode to episode, unerringly pointing to the miseries of contemporary Britain, such as, for example, the "umbrage of the New Left" (Larsen 2015: 106) in Scene Four and monetary policies in Scene Two, in which "[o]nce Arthur is rebuffed, and rebuffed again, the audience if not Ar-

thur understands that this isn't the world of medieval ro-
mances—it's the world of balances of payment deficits and a
belatedly, devastatingly devalued pound" (2015: 61). The
Great Britain portrayed in the film is not an immediate parody of clichéd, conventional imagery from the Breton cycle or
from Malory's take on the Arthurian quest; it is a densely wo-
ven fabric in which each sign is an interface communicating
between the England emerging from the survey carried out
through the *Domesday Book* and its contemporary version.

The strategy adopted by the dubbers resulted in a general simplification if not deliberate removal of the semiotical-
ly marked material with the aggravating circumstance of a
reductionist approach in terms of socio-historical specificity.
Alternate approaches could have included (a) a drastic trans-
figuration of said markers to create mental images and interpretants easily relatable to similar issues recognizable by
an Italian audience, or (b) a concise, controlled neutralization—according to Gottlieb (1998: 247), "condensation will
enhance rather than impair the effectiveness of the intended
message"—aimed at universalizing the recurring social, political and economic issues presented in the film, thereby
providing a successful, functionalist template for similar artifacts. Instead, the pervasive regionalization of the characters and the use of sport commentators for several connecting passages turned the Italian version of *MPHG* into an un-
recognizable, monstrous hybrid where the original humor
was replaced by heavy-handed caricatures, each Python
member and his complex spectrum of references supplanted
by the sophomoric jokes and the regional cadence of a character actor. It is an embarrassment dictated by a fundamental misunderstanding of the source, as Audissino (2016: 110)
writes about Scene 32 when the party encounters Tim the
Enchanter:

In the Italian version—besides King Arthur speaking with a Tuscan accent and Tim the Enchanter with a Neapolitan accent—there is a plethora of cheap and dated jokes on accountancy and tax matters that fill all the silent moments, as driven by a sort of logorrheic horror vacui that annihilates the surrealistic silence of the original.

Each scene is replete with conspicuous instances illustrating the ideological problems highlighted by Audissino. Here is an excerpt from Scene 6, with Arthur and Patsy running into the Black Knight and then Arthur chopping off all of his limbs:

English script	Italian version, delivered with a heavy Milanese accent	Back translation
BLACK KNIGHT: All right, we'll call it a draw.	BLACK KNIGHT: Guarda che bel taglio: mettiamo su una fabbrichetta di tranciatrici? O ci buttiamo negli affettati, eh? Salmone olandese…	BLACK KNIGHT: Look at this nice cut: shall we start a little factory of shearing machines? Or should we give cold cuts a try, eh? Dutch salmon…
ARTHUR: Come, Patsy.	ARTHUR: Andiamo.	ARTHUR: Let's go.
BLACK KNIGHT: Oh, oh, I see. Running away, eh? *You yellow bastards!* Come back here and take what's coming to ya! I'll bite y' legs off!	BLACK KNIGHT: …bologna sottovuoto! 30 ore settimanali, cassa integrazione al 98%! Guarda che l'artigianato va a rotoli! Non c'ha il bernoccolo degli affari, pirla!	BLACK KNIGHT: …vacuum-sealed bologna! Thirty-hour work week, Wages Guarantee Fund at ninety-eight %! Look, handicraft is going south! He doesn't have a head for business, the dimwit!

Massimilano Morini spoke of a "complete intertextual locative transfer" by virtue of which "the Arthurian story is a mere pretext for creating regional caricatures and alluding to Italian contemporary matters" (2012: 139). The arbitrary modification of the source material discredits the attempt at bringing attention to such matters as entrepreneurship, workers' rights, and so on, here deployed as mere props for a loud pantomime whose lasting impression will result from the Milanese overcharge of the locutionary act. The paradox is that in the case of *MPHG*, dubbing does not serve the primary purpose of indigenizing a foreign culture as much as erasing quite a number of extratextual, semiotic markers that do not simply corroborate the comedic material but construct an Arthurian image deeply grounded in coeval debates about the direction of an emasculated Britain. The Italian version of *MPHG* actually goes even further in its creative ways of perverting the source. The soothsayer who we encounter first in Scene 24, "The tale of Sir Launcelot scene," and then in Scene 35, "The bridge of death," is dubbed by Pippo Franco, and he does not shy from transforming the soothsayer's speeches and questions into a personal performance of Pippo Franco the entertainer from the Bagaglino theater company, with his own mannerisms, falsettos, and even catchphrases such as his trademark *praticamente no* (*practically no*). Such invasive interventions make the Target Version of *MPHG* a case study in how to maliciously neutralize interaction and how to mark fruition with a form of self-inflicted orientalism.

The arbitrary overloading of locutionary acts with dialectal overtones continued in two films directed by Stephen Chow, *Shaolin Soccer* (2001) and *Kung Fu Hustle* (2004), the first with the additional injury of entrusting the Italian version to a group of nonprofessionals, the second with a shameful colonization of the Cantonese language via racial trivialization. Thanks to its deep integration of the translating process into the target cultural systems, and to the itemization of aspects such as "production, consumption and market-related activities, as well as the relationship of negotiation between norms" (Agost 2004: 66), Díaz Cintas' Poly-system Theory (via Toury's Descriptive System) successfully accounts for the acts of erasure occurring in the films. Chow's comedies of underdogs, although apparently quite linear and unproblematic on the surface, do not shy from referencing contemporary events such as Asia's financial crisis of 2001 and hint at the courage and resilience of Hong Kong citizens when confronted with mainland Chinese rule in 1999. The filmmaker reminisces about the splendor of the sword-fighting genre and at the same time celebrates work-ing-class — or totally destitute — heroes by providing an escape from their pitiful conditions via a rediscovery of Hong Kong's cinematic roots of *wuxia* and martial arts, the creation of a cinematic universe where "the fantasmatic is taken for granted, as a lived cultural tradition (Shaolin and Wudang martial arts)" (Lee 2009: 128).

Chow is also not afraid of adopting an earthy, coarse aesthetics of worn-out objects and battered, ungraceful bodies caught during painful journeys of self-(re)discovery and redemption. As Chi-Keung wrote in regard to *Kung Fu Hustle*, "[b]y placing the marginal at the centre, the film essentially suggests to the audience that it is not necessary to follow the conventional definition of what is marginal; by displaying the hidden power of the excluded, it reminds them that power is not necessarily in the hands of those at the centre" (2009: 209). Again, the Italian distributor chose to strike the final blow on an already agonized body, the international, Miramax version — 20 minutes shorter than the Hong Kong version and the director's cut — which removes the introductory scene completely and waters down the intensity of many other ones. One could magnanimously forgive Carlo Vanzina's lisp and Romanesque accent in the annoying voiceover, which, by focusing almost exclusively on the protagonist-coach, meddles unnecessarily with the us-against-the-world narrative arc. What is unforgivable, though, even with the film's success at the box office as a goal, was the choice to entrust the voices of Fung's team to actual soccer players from AS Rome and Lazio, and to grossly regionalize bit pieces and even some more prominent roles and conversations with dialects from Apulia, Calabria, Campania, Lombardia, Sardinia, Sicily, Emilia, and Tuscany. The decimation continued with the orientalized dubbing of *Kung Fu*, in which the vibrating consonant "r" is loosely replaced by the liquid "l" in an operation aimed at neutralizing the source language and culture, equivalent to the disgraceful, grotesque *sì buana* type of dubbing — verbs used without conjugation, dehumanizing pronunciation, and so on — imposed on African and African-American characters until the 1960s. Albeit excessive in their fraudulent, relentless homogenization of other cultures, cases like the ones examined in this paragraph are exemplary of a certain tendency to cater to audiences whose knowledge of foreign nations is rudimentary at best. Going back to Raffaelli's observation, one cannot help but wonder how the practice of dubbing the near-totality of the films distributed in the Italian territory has exacerbated such lack of intellectual curiosity.

4. PHILOLOGICAL RESPECT AND SUCCESS CASES

Even when the dubbing refrains from ideological choices and seems to purposefully serve the source material, nuanced jokes and humorous situations may get lost in translation. The main concern is that there seems to be an almost irresistible temptation to slide toward clichéd and hackneyed representations even when the Target Texts maintain a respectful approach throughout. Such is the case, for example, of the versioning of John Landis' *The Kentucky Fried*

Movie (1977) whose strategies of compensation otherwise do a fine job of conveying a particular strand of parodic and demented humor. In the Italian version, unimaginatively entitled *Ridere per ridere* (literally: *to laugh for the sake of laughing*), one can find brilliant solutions such as the following phonetic adaptation and preservation of the original pun:

English script, from the episode "A Fistful of Yen"	Italian version	Back translation
ASQUITH: This is Butkus, Klahn's bodyguard. He is tough and ruthless. This is Kwong, Klahn's chauffeur. He is tough and toothless.	ASQUITH: Questo è Butkus, guardia del corpo di Klahn. Violento e senza morale. Questo è Kwong, autista di Klahn. Violento e senza molari.	ASQUITH: This is Butkus, Klahn's bodyguard. Violent and moral-less. This is Kwong, Klahn's chauffeur. Violent and molarless.

In *The Kentucky Fried Movie*, we also find a creative but very effective compensation adopted to preserve the original, "badass" character of a toy robot wreaking havoc in the compound that the hero is supposed to secure. The toy robot at first seems just a distraction that the hero is deploying to advance deeper into the compound, only to reveal its lethal potential before proceeding to shoot and kill the technician. The Italian version also adds an additional layer of expectation thanks to the intonation of the actor playing the technician, approaching the toy robot with the tenderness and curiosity one would use with a puppy or a baby.

English script, from the episode "A Fistful of Yen"	Italian version	Back translation
TECHNICIAN: A toy robot?	TECHNICIAN: Da dove vieni, robottino?	TECHNICIAN: Where are you from, little toy robot?
TOY ROBOT: Eat lead, sucker! (*The toy robot proceeds to gun down the technician.*)	TOY ROBOT: Sono cazzetti miei, stronzone!	TOY ROBOT: It's my little fucking business, big asshole!

Unfortunately, the suspension of disbelief—toward the quality of the Italian version, that is—is broken when the "game show host" testing the devotion of Klahn's guards with *Dating Game*-type questions is dubbed with a cadence resembling that of famous Italian-American TV host Mike Bongiorno, an extremely popular figure in Italian households for his quasi-monopoly on quiz shows during the early stages of national television. Examples from the movies analyzed above show the alarming trend of recurring to "specific culture-bound schemata" (Iaia 2015: 12) to shrink the field of interpretation and lead the audience to a safe territory of—allegedly shared—stereotypes.

On the other hand, *South Park: Bigger, Longer & Uncut* (1999) can be hailed as a virtuous example of versioning, with a few notable exceptions.

English script	Italian version	Back translation
STAN MARSH: You guys, do you know where I can find the clitoris?	STAN MARSH: Ehi, sapete dove posso trovare il clitoride?	STAN MARSH: Hey, do you know where I can find the clitoris?
KYLE BROFLOVSKI: The what?	KYLE BROFLOVSKI: Il che?	KYLE BROFLOVSKI: The what?
ERIC CARTMAN: Wait, is that like finding Jesus or something?	ERIC CARTMAN: Hai provato a chiedere al meccanico di tuo padre?	ERIC CARTMAN: Have you tried asking your father's mechanic?

It's unclear why the dubbers, in an altogether excellent translation, did not choose to go all the way and keep the spirit of the joke, based on misunderstanding and consequent mis-placement: the joke about the male gynecologist who is like a mechanic who has never owned a car seems a far-fetched translation for an Italian audience. A solution like "Cos'è, forse come trovare la fede?" ("What is it, perhaps like finding faith?") would have preserved the original structure via a smooth cultural adaptation, still embedding the joke into a religious background. The *South Park* movie also presents two additional challenges: the rendition of the songs, which in the Italian version are wisely left untouched—albeit entailing some additional confusion in instances where words and expressions recurring in the songs were transformed in the TV series, such as the school counselor's mantra "m'kay," which becomes "'pito" in Italian—and the accented English spoken by the Canadian officials in the United Nations scene. The latter problem was also approached in a dubious fashion, opting for a wordplay based on assonance—the Italian word "scòpo," which means "goal" or "aim" or "target" but is also very similar to "scópo," which is the first person of the verb *scopare*, which means to screw or to fuck. However, the pun gets lost in translation because there is no appreciable difference in the pronunciation of the same word by the American U.N. ambassador.

English script	Italian version	Back translation
U.N. CANADIAN AMBASSADOR: The fuss is *aboot* taking our citizens! It's *aboot* not censoring our art! It's *aboot*... It's *aboot*... (*other diplomats laugh*) What's so goddamn funny?	U.N. CANADIAN AMBASSADOR: Lo scopo è proteggere i nostri cittadini! Lo scopo è non censurare l'arte! Lo scopo... Lo scopo... (*I delegati ridono*) Che avete da ridere?	U.N. CANADIAN AMBASSADOR: The goal is to protect our citizens! The goal is to not censor art! The goal... The goal... What's so funny you have to laugh about it?
U.S. DIPLOMAT: Nothing, nothing. Could you tell us again what your argument is all about?	U.S. DIPLOMAT: Niente, niente. Potrebbe dirci di nuovo il vostro intento, il vostro scopo?	U.S. DIPLOMAT: Nothing, nothing. Could you tell us again your aim, your goal?
CANADIAN DIPLOMAT: This is not *aboot* diplomacy, this is *aboot* dignity! This is *aboot* respect! This is *aboot* realizing that humor... (*The entire Assembly laughs*) You guys are dicks! Release Terrance and Phillip or we'll give you something to cry *aboot*!	CANADIAN DIPLOMAT: Lo scopo non è la diplomazia, lo scopo è la dignità! Lo scopo è il rispetto! Lo scopo è capire che l'umorismo... (*L'intera Assemblea ride*) Liberate Trombino e Pompadour o il nostro scopo sarà farvi piangere!	CANADIAN DIPLOMAT: The goal is not diplomacy, the goal is dignity! The goal is respect! The goal is realizing that humor.... Free Trombino and Pompadour or our goal will be making you cry!

The stratagem works very poorly also because in the Italian version it is the American ambassador who first pronounces "scòpo" with no appreciable difference from his Canadian counterpart. A Frenchified Italian would have not been out of place, possibly insisting on the mispronunciation of words, in a way not dissimilar from the Italian Peter Sellers/Clouseau renditions. It is a faux pas in an altogether excellent version, in which the Italian dubbers had a field day intensifying the scatological references, specifically in the U.S. troops sequences: Terrance and Phillip as *Trombino e Pompadour*, names modeled from crude expressions describing sexual acts; Saddam interrupting the American general with a more graphic *V'inchiappetto!* ("I'll bugger you!" instead of "I'm coming to get you!"); Mr. Garrison's "dialogue" with Mr. Hat also being reinforced with more explicit sexual imagery; and finally, the crazy general retorting to Ted, *"Canadesi, Australiani, che cazzo ce ne frega?"* ("Canadians, Australian, who gives a fuck?")—a more forceful solution than "Canadians, Australian, what's the difference?" The case of the Italian version *South Park: Bigger, Longer & Uncut* seems a healthy exercise in surrogation; i.e. a controlled injection of profanities reinforcing the already strong foundations of the film, namely the absurdity of many traits of American culture as well as "the dangerous consequences of censorship and the importance of free speech" (Boyd and Plamondon 2008: 61).

5. CONCLUSION: TAKING HUMOR OUT OF THE PROVINCIAL

If audiovisual translation fluctuates between "its adequacy to the source text and its accessibility within the target culture" (Marzà i Ibàñez and Chaume Varela 2009: 33), the biggest problems seem to arise when an ill-advised anxiety to satisfy the latter disfigures the source and transforms it into a monstrous hybrid, trying to turn *Shaolin Soccer* into a vehicle for Italian soccer players or *MPHG* into a dialectal parody of regional fairs, thereby freezing the dynamic cores of the source and removing the audience from a complete form of enjoyment. But even "neutral" approaches, successful at conveying the majority of the jokes at the risk of dubbers taking a symbolic step back and simply working with accepted variants often neutralize some of the most powerful jokes. A case in point is *Galaxy Quest* (1999), sort of *Star Trek* spoof in which the cast of a space-set science fiction series are forced to play their roles for real when an alien race, whose devotion is based on misinterpreting the show as actual stellar exploration, calls for their help. *Galaxy Quest* is extremely versatile at finding ways to elicit laughter, and when the humor is generated by slapstick and reflexive gags taking on the genre and the world of fandom surrounding it the Italian version is accurate and serviceable in terms of pragmatics and semantics. Problems arise when the dubber is not as subtle as the actor in the original. Case in point: the out-of-his-depth technician, masterfully played by Tony Shalhoub, whose rich palette of insecurities, wild guesses or complete unpreparedness is reduced to a deadpan delivery in Italian that does not capture the constant state of tension he is in.

By the same token, the Spock surrogate Alexander Dane, played by Alan Rickman, also comes across as a shallower version because of the neutralization of his British accent and consequently of his disdain for a form of entertainment perceived as infinitely less noble than Shakespearean theater. Dubbing practices when translating into Italian are problematic enough — the Romanesque accent, the redundant and uncalled for sentimental tone, etc. — and the additional problem of versioning humor can turn them into something outright catastrophic. According to Toury's (1995) descriptive model, if the target text is the dynamic hybridization of two or more cultures in dialogue or conflict, then the more traits said cultures will have in common and the more loyal the version will be. For instance, in *Analyze This* (1999) by Harold Ramis there is a scene in which the two protagonists—a mafia boss named Paul Vitti played by Robert De Niro and a psychiatrist named Ben Sobel played by Billy Crystal—are taped by the FBI while walking on the Miami beach. Crystal's character is simply a counselor and not a crime partner or consultant for De Niro who is going through a life crisis, but the FBI agent speculates that he must be "Vitti's new *consigliere*." Here, Italy's expertise and sheer body of work on mafia comes in handy because the Target Version adds a witty twist by translating the sentence into "dev'essere il nuovo *consigliori* di Vitti," a word that can be used in humorous ways and indirectly refers to an eponymous film made in 1973. However, if Italian creativity with scurrility works wonders in the cases of *The Kentucky Fried Movie* and *South Park*, it is detrimentally orientalist in *MPHG*—possibly sound as a business decision but coercive in its erasure of the specifically British socio-historical wealth one can find in the works of Monty Python.

REFERENCES

Adab, Beverly. "Interlingual Dubbing, Characterization and Identity: a Functionalist Framework with Insights from Peircean Semiotics." *Translating Voices, Translating Regions.* Eds. Armstrong, Nigel and Federico M. Federici. Rome: Aracne, 2006. 183-206.

Agost Canós, Rosa. *Traducción i Doblaje: Palabras, Voces, Imágenes.* Barcelona: Ariel, 1999.

_____. "Translation in Bilingual Contexts: Different Norms in Dubbing Translation." *Topics in Audiovisual Translation.* Ed. Pilar Orero. Amsterdam & Philadelphia: John Benjamins, 2004. 61-82.

Analyze This. Dir. Harold Ramis. Village Roadshow Pictures. 1999.

Audissino, Emilio. "Dubbing as a Formal Interference: Reflections and Examples." *Media and Translation: An Interdisciplinary Approach.* Ed. Dror Abend-David. New York & London: Bloomsbury, 2016. 97-118.

Boyd, Jason and Marc R. Plamondon. "Orphic Persuasions and Siren Seductions: Vocal Music in *South Park*." *Taking South Park Seriously.* Ed. Jeffrey Andrew Weinstock. Albany: SUNY Press, 2008. 59-78.

Chi-Keung, Yam. "A Secular Gospel for the Marginal: Two Films of Stephen Chow as Hong Kong Cinematic Parables." *Exploring Religion and the Sacred in a Media Age.* Eds. Deacy, Christopher and Elisabeth Arweck. Farnham and Burlington: Ashgate, 2009. 203-218.

Delabastita, Dirk. "Focus On the Pun: Wordplay As a Special Problem in Translation Studies." *Target: International Journal On Translation Studies,* 6.2. 1994. 223-243.

Díaz Cintas, Jorge. "In Search of a Theoretical Framework for the Study of Audiovisual Translation." *Topics in Audiovisual Translation.* Ed. Pilar Orero. Amsterdam & Philadelphia: John Benjamins, 2004. 21-34.

Ferrari, Chiara. "Translating Stereotypes: Local and Global in Italian Television Dubbing." *Translating Voices, Translating Regions.* Eds. Armstrong, Nigel and Federico M. Federici. Rome: Aracne, 2006. 123-142.

Gambier, Yves. "Introduction: Screen Transadaptation: Perception and Reception." *The Translator – Studies in Intercultural Communication,* 9.2. 2003. 171-189.

Gottlieb, Henrik. "Subtitling." *Routledge Encyclopedia of Translation Studies.* Ed. Mona Baker. London & New York: Routledge, 1998. 244-248.

Guido, Maria Grazia. *The Acting Translator: Embodying Cultures in the Dubbing Translation of American Sitcoms.* New York and Ottawa: Legas, 2012.

Hatim, Basil and Ian Mason. *Discourse and the Translator.* London: Longman, 1990.

Iaia, Pietro Luigi. *The Dubbing Translation of Humorous Audiovisual Texts.* Newcastle upon Tyne: Cambridge Scholars, 2015.

Jakobson, Roman. "On Linguistic Aspects of Translation." *On Translation*. Ed. Reuben A. Brower. Cambridge, Mass.: Harvard University Press, 1959. 232-239. Reprint New York: Galaxy Books, 1966.

Kung Fu Hustle. Dir. Stephen Chow. Columbia Pictures Film Production Asia. 2004.

Larsen, Darl. *A Book About the Film* Monty Python and the Holy Grail*: All References from African Swallows to Zoot*. Lanham: Rowman & Littlefield, 2015.

Lee, Vivian P.Y. *Hong Kong Cinema Since 1997: The Post-Nostalgic Imagination*. Basingstoke and New York: Palgrave Macmillan, 2009.

Marzà i Ibàñez, Anna and Frederic Chaume Varela. "The Language of Dubbing: Present Facts and Future Perspectives." *Analysing Audiovisual Dialogue: Linguistic and Translational Insights*. Eds. Pavesi, Maria and Maria Freddi. Bologna: CLUEB, 2009. 32-40.

Mereu Keating, Carla. *The Politics of Dubbing: Film Censorship and State Intervention in the Translation of Foreign Cinema in Fascist Italy*. Bern: Peter Lang, 2016.

Monty Python and the Holy Grail. Dir. Terry Gilliam and Terry Jones. Michael White Productions. 1975.

Morini, Massimiliano. *The Pragmatic Translator: An Integral Theory of Translation*. New York & London: Bloomsbury, 2012.

Paolinelli, Mario and Eleonora Di Fortunato. *Tradurre per il doppiaggio. La trasposizione linguistica dell'audiovisivo: teoria e pratica di un'arte imperfetta*. Milano: Hoeply, 2005.

Raffaelli, Sergio. "L'italiano dei film doppiati." *Premio Città di Monselice per la traduzione letteraria e scientifica*. Ed. Gianfelice Peron. Monselice: Il Poligrafo, 2004. 63-73.

Shaolin Soccer. Dir. Stepehn Chow. Star Overseas. 2001.

Sisto, Antonella. *Film Sound in Italy: Listening to the Screen*. New York: Palgrave Macmillan, 2014.

South Park: Bigger, Longer & Uncut. Dir. Trey Parker. Scott Rudin Productions. 1999.

The Kentucky Fried Movie. Dir. John Landis. KFM Films. 1977.

Toury, Gideon. *Descriptive Translation Studies and Beyond*. Amsterdam & Philadelphia: John Benjamins, 1995.

Venuti, Lawrence. *The Translator's Invisibility: A History of Translation*. London & New York: Routledge, 1995.

Zabalbeascoa, Patrick. "Translating Jokes for Dubbed Television Situation Comedies." *The Translator – Studies in Intercultural Communication* 2.2. 1996. 235-257.

Dubbing in Advanced Italian Courses

Felice Italo Beneduce

The purpose of this essay will be the examination of the use of dubbing analysis and redubbing as pedagogical instruments in my Advanced Italian Courses at Columbia University as well as to provide fellow language instructors a pedagogical tool that I have found exceptionally effective. The study of the cultural fluidity and hybridity that dubbing represents constitutes in my courses the basis for a contextualized review of advanced grammatical functions as well as the presentation of aspects of Italian culture which dubbing brings to the forefront. This is particularly true in Italy which has historically promoted dubbing over subtitling (in cinema and television) thereby introducing national characteristics through what Chiara Ferrari has defined as "cultural ventriloquism" (Ferrari 2010: 29).

Advanced Italian at Columbia is a series of 5th semester courses designed for students who are majoring in Italian or wish to improve their linguistic skills beyond the intermediate level (4th semester). The Italian Department offers Advanced Italian in a variety of sections: Advanced Italian I and II, Advanced Conversation, Learning Italian in Class Online: A Telecollaboration With Italy and Advanced Italian Through Cinema. In this article, I will focus my attention on the Advanced Italian Through Cinema course and the relevant position dubbing has assumed in it in recent years[1]. Among the

---

[1] I first became interested in the use of dubbing in my pedagogy thanks to my collaboration with Luke Rosenau of Columbia University, to whom I am very

most stimulating and meaningful projects I have undertaken since my arrival at Columbia University in 2010 has been the re-writing of the Advanced Italian Through Cinema syllabus. Prior to coming to Columbia, I had never taught a cinema-based language course, yet, while a somewhat formidable endeavor, I enthusiastically accepted the challenge to redevelop the syllabus. Simultaneously, the need for a diversification of material has consistently led me to employ an array of technologies which are instrumental for an educator in the development of exercises that encourage discussion, critical thinking and, ultimately, student participation. While I firmly believe that the application of technology has the potential to enhance the quality of foreign language teaching, I am left somewhat perplexed by recent tendencies to utilize new technology apparently for technology's sake (e.g. the current infatuation with Prezi). I feel that the *effectiveness* of the technology must take center stage, therefore I have supplemented my lectures with technological tools that have proven especially beneficial to my classes and have facilitated the comprehension of the material for my students. Up to date, the most effective of these audio-visual technologies have ranged from programs for the creation an original work of Sequential Art to precisely the analysis of dubbing and the inventive redubbing of classic scenes from the history of American cinema. The fundamental premise of the new syllabus was the transformation of the cinema component: rather than merely a source of reactive language activities, I redirected the focus of the syllabus towards the creation of language through the creation of cinema, centered on several group projects distributed throughout the semester, two of which revolve around dubbing. My students examine the complex linguistic and

---

grateful for the suggestions and material.

socio-cultural processes of dubbing that create, intentionally or unintentionally, new relationships of meaning and the role of the translator in the dissemination of these relationships.

The introduction to dubbing takes place as a preliminary in-class discussion regarding the students' opinions on the topic. I start by asking my students if they prefer dubbed or subtitled films and the reasons for their choice. Invariably, a preference emerges for subtitles which afford students the possibility to enjoy the film in the original language. In the next stage, the class investigates the differences which may exist between dubbing and subtitle translation and what the advantages of each may be. My goal at this point is to elicit from the students the issue of synchronization, which I insist should be a major point in their subsequent analyses and projects.

I then present to the class two sets of non-Italian actors who are dubbed into Italian. The students view the same scene twice: first with the actor's original voice and then the dubbed version. The first group is comprised of French actors who appear dubbed in Italian films: Fernandel in *Don Camillo* (Duvivier, 1952), Jean-Louis Trintignant in *Il sorpasso* (Risi, 1962) and Philippe Noiret in *Nuovo Cinema Paradiso* (Tornatore, 1988). I define this first group as "soft" comparisons since most students are not familiar with these actors therefore classroom analyses can concentrate on the differences between the voices and, with Don Camillo[2] and Alfredo,[3] the topic of regional accents used in dubbing, a theme which will return later in the semester. I then pass to "shock" comparisons, i.e. the presentation of iconic scenes or actors from English speaking films with which students are typically familiar, alongside their Italian-

---

[2] Don Camillo also allows for a brief excursus on the politics of translation; specifically how the first English translations in the 1950s introduced significant modifications to Guareschi's original in order to emphasize the dangers of communism (Venuti 2002: 142-150).

[3] Alfredo is the character played by Philippe Noiret in *Nuovo Cinema Paradiso*.

dubbed counterparts. My selections include: John Wayne[4] from *The Searchers* (Ford, 1956); the "I am your father" scene from *Star Wars: Episode V – The Empire Strikes Back* (Lucas, 1980);[5] and finally the Bridge of Khazad-dûm scene from *The Lord of the Rings: The Fellowship of the Ring* (Jackson, 2001). The immediate reaction for this second group is always laughter which leads to a discussion of the reasons that underlay this laughter and the characteristic of dubbing to undermine expectations. The examination of these scenes represents the first approach of my students towards the comparative analyses which they will have to present for their midterm projects.

I next provide an overview of dubbing's historical context in Italian cinema. This overview includes the study of multi-language versions (MLV) of the same film from the 1920s and 1930s which represented Hollywood's attempt to secure the European market. The options American producers adopted were either to shoot a foreign language version of the film in the United States with foreign-born actors or to reshoot the film in production facilities constructed in Europe (Vincendau 1988: 24). In class, I show parallel scenes from *The Big Trail* (Walsh, 1930) and *Il grande sentiero* (Loeffler & Walsh, 1931) as well as from *The Devil's Holiday* (Goulding, 1930) and *La vacanza del diavolo* (Salvatori, 1931). Since these are not *dubbed* but *translated* scenes, clearly synchronization is not a relevant factor and the class can devote greater attention to the manner in which the scenes are reshot and the quality of the translations per se.

---

[4] Sometimes substituted with Clint Eastwood from *The Good, the Bad and the Ugly* (Leone, 1966).

[5] The scene also is conducive to a discussion of the impositions of cultural factors on translation e.g. the choice to rename Vader as Fener, dictated by the resemblance of the original name with the word "*water*" (toilet) in Italian.

Nancy Carroll and Phillips Holmes in *The Devil's Holiday* (Edmund Goulding, 1930)	Carmen Boni and Maurizio D'Ancora in *La vacanza del diavolo* (Jack Salvatori, 1931)
Franco Corsaro and Luisa Caselotti in *Il grande sentiero* (Louis Loeffler & Roul Walsh, 1931)	John Wayne and Marguerite Churchill in *The Big Trail* (Roul Walsh, 1930)

Figure 1

The class then examines some of the more intriguing aspects of Italian dubbing from the 1930s to the 1950s. The mandatory dubbing of foreign films enacted by the Fascist government in the 1930s was intrinsically connected to one of the Regime's foremost linguistic policies: the dissemination of standard Italian as the national language throughout the peninsula. During this period, for many Italians, dubbed films were a primary source of contact with the standard of their national language, an Italian purged of any regional accent or inflection deriving from dialect. Many residents of the peninsula learned to use this national language not thanks to the State or the school system but, paradoxically, thanks to the dubbed voices of American actors (Bachelloni 1997: 438).

Another feature of this period analyzed in class is the need to adapt or *domesticate* American films to an Italian context which at times led to questionable translation choices, e.g. the decision to Italianize the names of characters. For instance, in *Father of the Bride* (Minnelli, 1950) Spencer Tracey's character Stanley becomes Sandro while Elizabeth Taylor's Kay becomes Carla. I also introduce the sociolinguistic complexities which emerge when the original presents a variety of non-standard language jargons, registers or varieties of colloquialisms that refer to particular characters or social strata (Diadori 2003: 533). A markedly execrable example is represented by the dubbing of African American English in the case of Mammy from *Gone with the Wind*. When the film was first dubbed into Italian in 1950, all the African American actors spoke in a heavily accented, ungrammatical Italian of limited vocabulary and all verbs in the infinitive[6], an instance of overt racism which was only rectified in 1977 when the film was redubbed with the non-white actors speaking standard Italian.

Finally, I present to the class examples of exceptionally ingenious solutions in dubbing multi-lingual pieces i.e. scenes in which instances of bilingualism or plurilingualism emerge. I explain to my students that in these cases dialogue writers may adopt different strategies (Diadori 2003: 340), the first of which is leave the foreign piece unchanged, either with or without subtitles. Clearly, this is not a viable option when the

---

[6] E.g. "Ze a te non importare buona rebutazione, a me zì...Quello che giovanotti dire e quello che pensare ezere due coze."

"foreign language" of the original coincides with the Target Language of the dubbing. The students view such an example of the difficulties of dubbing taken from *La vita è bella* (Benigni, 1997), specifically the scene in which Benigni translates the orders of the German soldier to the newcomers in the lager dormitory. As Diadori (2003: 335) recalls, the version of the film dubbed into German had to resort the artifice of leaving the Italian voice of Benigni (which in the rest of the film is dubbed) and subtitling this scene in German: only in this way could the spectator grasp the comic discrepancy between the original orders and the translation made by the protagonist of the film.

A second option for the dialogue writers is to resort to different expedients to conserve the bilingualism or plurilingualism of the original. Among these expedients are the insertion of foreign words into the dialogue, though absent from the original, or the attribution of a foreign accent to characters. In this specific case, the class examines scenes in which spoken Italian is present in the original English film e.g. *A Fish Called Wanda* (Crichton, 1988) or *Inglorious Basterds* (Tarantino, 2009). In *Fish*, the dialogue writers transform Kevin Kleins's tourist-dictionary Italian into Spanish while in Tarantino's film Brad Bitt's barely intelligible Italian becomes Sicilian. The second example is an indication of a tendency within the Italian dubbing industry to resort to regional Italian also for comedic effect. I present in class a further instance of this tendency with clips taken from *The Simpsons* in which Groundskeeper Willie is dubbed with a Sardinian accent, Reverend Lovejoy with Calabrese and Carl with Venetian. In order to convey the differences of pronunciation, I provide students with extracts of *The Simpsons* lines after which then they hear the characters enunciate those lines.

Once this preparatory phase is completed, I then organize actual dubbing analyses through the examination of specific scenes in English and Italian. The first of these, in conjunction with the widespread use of regional accents in Italian dubbing, leads me to a reflection on language instruction, one of the mantras of which over the past decades has been the need to use "authentic" material. During my career, I have employed realia to present in my classroom an authentic portrait of Italian culture that transcends the postcard depictions all too common in Italian language courses. In other words, I present to my students a 360° portrait of Italy, both positive and negative, from which they subsequently draw their own conclusions. Simultaneously, I have also begun to question what realia means and, iconoclastically, I have inserted into my courses material which traditionally language courses have excluded because deemed "inauthentic" i.e. dubbing. In my experience, however, the exact opposite has proven to be true and the conveyance of a sense of plural authenticity to my students through dubbing has assumed an increasingly important role in my language teaching. In this light, the first scene examined in the classroom is a piece which I believe inherently exemplifies this plural authenticity of realia: the Bonasera monologue that opens Francis Ford Coppola's *The Godfather* (1972). This plurality stems from the fact that Arturo Domenici, who dubs Salvatore Corsitto (Amerigo Bonasera), does so with a marked Sicilian accent which preserves intact the authenticity of an encounter between two Sicilians living in New York in the 1940s. This approach, at the time revolutionary, concerning the dubbing of *The Godfather* instituted long-lasting practices regarding how Italian American accents should be portrayed in Italian dubbing. The dialogue writers opted for the rejection of a national language which was to a considerable extent artificial in favor of linguistic modes that reflected the interstitial reality of Italian Americans, so as to emphasize the distinct ethnicity and psychological characteristics of Italian American characters in relation to Italy (Paolinelli and Di Fortunato 2005: 19).

> L'America fece la mia fortuna. E io crescevo mia figlia come un'americana. E ci detti libertà ma ci insegnavo pure a non disonorare la famiglia. Lei aveva un "boyfriend," non italiano.

> [America has made my fortune. And I raised my daughter in the American fashion. I gave her freedom, but I taught her never to dishonor her family. She found a boyfriend, not an Italian].

As an in-class exercise, I have my students read the monologue transcribed into standard Italian and underline the words with which they are not familiar. They then listen to the dubbed scene and report the points that do not match to the Italian transcription. This occurs above all with a series of regionalisms Domenici and the translators introduced into the dialogue (*loro-iddi, mascella-mascidda, piangere-chiangere, più-chiù, presi-pigghiati*). These regionalisms not only confer upon the monologue a greater sense of realism but they also serve as a translingual compensation for Bonasera's heavily accented English (e.g. *a'broken, a'shattered*) which clearly is impossible to translate. On the one hand, by means of these regionalisms, the dialogue writers provide a linguistic authenticity to Bonasera which the original lacks; on the other, the writers also convey the sense of "Italian-Americanness," as it were, through the inclusion in the Italian version of English terms, e.g. "boyfriend." Finally, in class the students compare the two transcripts, report the points where the dubbing distances itself from the original and attempt to provide justifications for this distance. Since the scene is almost entirely shot as a close up of Bonasera, it allows for the introduction of synchronization as a primary factor of dubbing which very often demands a reconfiguration of the original dialogue in order to account for the movement of the actors' lips.

In the next phase of the course, the class then passes on to the comparative analyses of a dialogue in the original English and dubbed into Italian: the first dialogue is taken from *The Big Lebowski* (1998) directed by the Coen brothers, with Jeff Bridges, John Goodman and Steve Buscemi, specifically the bowling alley scene. I distribute a table with the two dialogues side by side (an excerpt is provided below). I assign each student a character and the class reads/acts out the scenes, first in English then in Italian, so the students may discern where the emphases lay and the pauses that the dialogue may require. The class examines the more difficult aspects of translation, both from a linguistic and cultural point of view, and engages in a brief translation exercise, having to determine which sentences seem easier to translate and which are more difficult (e.g. "I'm throwin' rocks tonight"). The class then views the two scenes on screen, after which group work on comparative analysis begins: the students must judge the quality of the dubbing, whether it changes the scene in any way, and what aspects of the original language the dubbing conserves or discards.

Among the points of discussion are: the elimination or reduction of profanity of the original version (lines d, f, g and h); the choice to change the name of Jeff Bridges' character from Dude to Drugo (line 1); and most importantly the translation of John Goodman's line "Also, Dude, Chinaman is not the preferred nomenclature... Asian-American. Please." (line l) which allows for analysis at a variety of levels. Firstly, I posit whether it represents a subdued criticism of the directors vis-à-vis the culture of political correctness in the United States. Secondly, and more significantly, the students comment on an historical context which is largely lost on Italians. Although not the most derogatory ethnic slur directed towards Chinese Americans, "Chinaman" has a very specific historical connotation that is impossible to transfer into Italian without lengthy explanations. The reference is to the large numbers of Chinese who came to the United States in the 1860s, recruited by the Central Pacific Railroad to complete the Transcontinental Railroad through the Sierra Nevada Mountains. While the Dude refers to this connotation by mentioning the railroads explicitly, the same reference in Italian falls flat for the average Italian viewer because there is no immediate connection between "ferrovie" and "muso giallo," (lines 13 and 12) potentially a more disparaging term in comparison to the original. (See APPENDIX, Figures 2a, 2b)

Another scene I present is the "Ezekiel" piece from Quentin Tarantino's *Pulp Fiction* (1994). Again, I provide my students with a comparative table of the two dialogues and the class follows the same procedure adopted with *The Big Lebowski*. In this case, the dialogue serves to emphasize to the students the intricacies of translation e.g. with the construction of the parallel rhymes *Pitt-shit, Gerda-merda*. Also of note is the substitution of *English* with *la mia lingua*: as I explain to my students, obviously, the Italian viewer will intuitively understand that Samuel L Jackson is speaking English but *la mia lingua* is an example of self-referential accommodations that dubbing must occasionally adopt in order to foreignize the dubbed scene to a certain extent. Lastly, I point out to my students the Protestant-Baptist preacher tone to the piece, lacking from Italian culture, but with which the Italian viewer may be familiar as a consequence of a decades-long to exposure to American cinema. (See APPENDIX, Figures 3a, 3b)

Once in-class analysis exercises have been concluded, the students begin preparation for their midterm project (20% of final grade), for which each student must prepare a comparative analysis of two dialogues: one in the original and the second of the same scene dubbed into Italian, the only limitation being that the language of the original must be English (thus allowing other students in the class to comment on the presenter's analysis). In preparation for these projects, the students begin to acquire the theoretical instruments with which they will conduct their analyses. The students' first step is to gauge the piece's translatability that Benjamin in "The Task of the Translator" defines as the expression of a "specific significance inherent in the original text" (Benjamin 2012: 76). I also introduce the class to the more common strategies (Sapino 2000: 200-213) employed in the translation of a script for the dubbed version of a film. I explain that the linguistic and cultural adaptation that this process entails is accomplished through a variety of approaches. Among the most important:

a. shift: the use of semantic changes that vary the intensity of the source text;

b. addition: the insertion of material absent in the original, especially when the character is off-screen, that is, in those moments when the requirements of synchronization are less prevalent;

c. clarification: the explanation of expressions referring to contexts and situations of the source language which may cause difficulty in comprehension;

d. cancellation: elision of words and expressions that refer to the culture of the film's source language, that may be unrelatable to the viewer.

The first step is the selection of a scene which has been dubbed and is readily available online. I suggest the students save the MP4s on hard drives, as there is a possibility that clips may suddenly be removed from websites such as

YouTube. For the project, the student must provide me with transcriptions of the two dialogues side by side, following the examples of in-class analyses described above. The purpose of this is to ensure the correct transcription of the Italian which, until quite recently, the students had to transcribe manually (over the past few years these scripts have become more readily available online).

In their oral presentation, the students present both scenes to the class and critically analyze the quality of the translation and the dubbing keeping in mind linguistic and cultural aspects of translation, the strategies adopted by the dialogue writers and the synchronization. In their analyses, students must determine whether the translator has successfully achieved the adaptation of a text which connects two disparate cultures, even though the original may be substantially modified in order to convey corresponding responses in the Target Language observer (Paolinelli and Di Fortunato 2005: 40). I require that my students determine whether the translator has resorted to one of two possible approaches a translator may adopt, as first posited by Lawrence Venuti. According to Venuti (2002: 20) the choices facing a translator are

> between a *domesticating method*, an ethnocentric reduction of the foreign text to target-language cultural values, bringing the author back home, and a *foreignizing method*, an ethnodeviant pressure on those values to register the linguistic cultural difference of the foreign text, sending the reader abroad.

The dubbing analysis project thus engages students on a variety of levels: firstly, it introduces them to the "art" of translation, thereby dismantling the stereotypes which have very often been associated with it in language teaching; secondly, the examination of the translated material helps to improve the lexical and grammatical abilities of the students.

The comparative analysis is also conducive to a reflection on metalinguistics: for example, the extent to which the constraints of labial synchronization impose limits on the choices of the translator; the adaptation of the subtle implications in certain modes of speech and accents; or how a culture-bound term may be rendered. Culture-bound terms cause certain difficulties of translation because effectively they have no equivalents in the Target Language cultural system (Hatim and Mason 1990: 223-224). According to Newmark (1988: 78) problems in translation caused by these terms derive from their intrinsic and unique connection to the Source Language culture and, therefore, are related to a context of a cultural tradition. Newmark categorizes these culture-specific items into five areas: (1) ecology (facets of nature), (2) material culture (food, clothing, abodes), (3) social culture (4) politics, religion or art, and (5) customs.

Following the premise that dubbing has the power to misrepresent and distort (Whitman-Linsen 1992: 11), for the final project (25% of final grade), I assign to groups of students a scene from one of the American Film Institutes' ten greatest films (e.g. *Citizen Kane, The Wizard of Oz, Raging Bull*), which they must *creatively rewrite*. I require them to base their new script primarily on the actors' lip movements but they must also distance themselves completely from the context of the original and incorporate humor into their new dialogue. I have found that these constraints stimulate the students' imagination, forcing them to find solutions that are exceptionally creative. As an example for the students, the class views the piece "Medieval Land Fun-Time World"[7] in which scenes from *Game of Thrones* are redubbed to create a preview clip of a fictitious film set in a medieval theme park. The park manager, Eddie

---

[7] https://www.youtube.com/watch?v=5Krz-dyD-UQ

Stark, has one week to whip his lackluster group of employees into shape before the park's grand opening. The quality of the translation and the synchronization is exceptional and includes elements of humor which students must include in their projects.

Each group presents their idea to the class for the other students to provide their input into the project. The group then writes a script which is corrected twice before recording. My recommendations for the recording are limited to: volume, which should be clearly audible but not overwhelming; the elimination of background noise; the speed of their enunciations, which should not be too fast and above all must adhere to synchronization of the actors which, as mentioned, places considerable limitations on the choice of lexical items if the utterance is to match the movement of the actors' lips; and finally the avoidance of overly specific terminology which would be incomprehensible to their classmates. For the technical aspect of the redubbing project, the actual creation of a new audio associated with the scene, the students use either IMovie or Moviemaker on their computers. Furthermore, I avail myself of the invaluable assistance of Columbia University's Language Resource Center which generously provides meaningful input and practical tutorials for my students. Following a presentation of the scene to the class, the students must then justify their selections. This final project allows students to engage in cultural ventriloquism which according to film scholar Antje Ascheid is invariably the creation of an entirely new entity. The students appropriate and recreate a new text for new characters which undergo fundamental shifts in the construction of their identity and context (Ascheid 1997).

A major pitfall I encountered emerged from a project redubbing a courtroom scene in *To Kill A Mockingbird* (Mulligan

1962), specifically when Atticus (Gregory Peck) is cross-examining Mayella (Collin Wilcox) as defense attorney for Tom (Brock Peters). The group, consisting in two female students, created an outstanding piece of redubbing, centering their new dialogue around the theft of a *panino*. Subsequently, however, they met with me privately to express their misgivings regarding the selection of the original scene. Since it dealt with a perceived rape, they questioned its appropriateness for inclusion in the course. Clearly, they were correct: in my enthusiasm to find scenes that lent themselves to redubbing, I had failed to take this into consideration and I have since eliminated the scene from my pool.

To conclude, in my attempt to have my students become more than passive recipients of the information presented to them in the lectures, I have increasingly focused my attention on specific fields which I have successfully melded into my syllabi and classroom pedagogy. One of the many innovations I have introduced to my courses is centered on translation. Since my background is originally in Translation Studies, I am glad to have had the opportunity to incorporate TS into my classroom. Moreover, I have devoted considerable time and effort to ensure that an emphasis on the artistic and creative expression of my students — which I feel has been rewarding both for myself and for them — is always at the center of my classes. In this light, dubbing has proven a particularly useful technological instrument in my Advanced Italian Through Cinema course and this innovative and successful addition to the course's traditional structure has allowed for the adoption of a much livelier and more effective approach to the teaching of Italian culture and language. Through the class projects, I have successfully elicited sophisticated reflections on the comparison of languages and cultures from my students. Consequently, dubbing has become instrumental for the primary purpose of these courses: to deepen and perfect students' knowledge of Italian language, both the written and spoken.

Appendix

1. Theodore Donald 'DONNY' Kerabatsos: *Sembro un cannone stasera*. Segna il punto, Drugo.	a. Theodore Donald 'DONNY' Kerabatsos: *I'm throwing rocks tonight*. Mark it, Dude.
2. WALTER SOBCHAK: Che schifo! E magari era un tappeto di valore. Cosa poteva... […]	b. WALTER SOBCHAK: This was a valued rug. This was a... […]
3. DRUGO: Walter, si può sapere dove vuoi arrivare?	c. DUDE: Walter, what's the point, man?
4. WALTER: Te lo dico subito: non c'è un motivo. Non c'è proprio nessun motivo per cui...	d. WALTER: There's no reason- here's my point, Dude...There's no **fucking** reason-
5. DONNY: Già, dove vuoi arrivare?	e. DONNY: Yeah, Walter, what's your point?
6. DRUGO: Walter, qual è il punto? Guarda, lo sappiamo tutti da che parte sta la ragione, e allora perché parli a vanvera?	f. DUDE: Walter, what is the point- Look, we all know who is at fault here. What the **fuck** are you talking about?
7. WALTER: Cosa? No, ma **vaffan**... Io non... Stiamo parlando di un'aggressione immotivata, *Drugo*.	g. WALTER: No, what the **fuck** are you- We're talking about unchecked aggression here, *Dude*.
8. DONNY: Si può sapere di che parla?	h. DONNY: What the **fuck** is he talking about?
9. DRUGO: Del mio tappeto.	i. DUDE: My rug.
10. WALTER: Non ti immischiare, Donny! Non è il tuo campo.	j. WALTER: Forget it, Donny. You're out of your element.
11. DRUGO: Walter. Walter! Non posso presentare il conto al *muso giallo* che mi ha pisciato sul tappeto. Si può sapere di che **cazzo** stai parlando?	k. DUDE: Walter, the *Chinaman* who peed on my rug, I can't go give him a bill. So what the **fuck** are you talking about?

Figure 2a

12. WALTER: Di che **cazzo** stai parlando tu! La questione qui non è il muso giallo! Io parlo di una linea tracciata sulla sabbia, Drugo. Se qualcuno la oltrepassa, tu non devi... *e poi scusa, "muso giallo" non mi sembra l'appellativo corretto per un cinese. "Asiatico" è preferibile.*	l. WALTER: What the **fuck** are you talking about? The Chinaman is not the issue here, Dude. I'm talking about drawing a line in the sand, Dude. Across this line, you do not- *Also, Dude, Chinaman is not the preferred nomenclature. Asian-American, please.*
13. DRUGO: Walter, non stiamo parlando di *uno che costruisce ferrovie,* quello è uno che...	m. DUDE: Walter, this isn't a guy who built the railroads here. This is a guy...

Figure 2b

1. JULES: We happy? Vincent! We happy?	a. JULES: Siamo contenti? Vincent? Siamo contenti?
2. VINCENT: Yeah. We're happy.	b. VINCENT: Sì, siamo contenti.
3. BRETT: Look, I'm sorry, I-I didn't get your name. I got yours, uh, Vincent, right? But-But I-I never got your...	c. BRETT: Ehm... ascolta... Mi dispiace, io... io... io non ho capito il tuo nome. Ho... ho capito il tuo, ehm, Vincent, giusto? Ma non ho capito il tuo.
4. JULES: *My name is Pitt, and your ass ain't talking your way outta this shit.* [...]	d. JULES: *Mi chiamo Gerda e non è con le chiacchiere che uscirai da questa merda.* [...]
5. JULES: What country are you from?	e. JULES: Da che paese vieni?
6. BRETT: Wha-what?	f. BRETT: Cosa? Cosa?
7. JULES: "What" ain't no country I ever heard of! They speak English in "What"!?	g. JULES: "Cosa" è un paese che non ho mai sentito nominare! Lì parlano la mia lingua?
8. BRETT: What?	h. BRETT: Cosa?

Figure 3a

9. JULES: English, **motherfucker**! Do you speak it!? […]	i. JULES: La mia lingua, **figlio di puttana**! Tu la sai parlare? […]
10.JULES: Well, there's this passage I've got memorized, sorta fits the occasion. Ezekiel 25:17? "The path of the righteous man is beset on all sides by the iniquities of the selfish and the tyranny of evil men. Blessed is he who in the name of charity and good will shepherds the weak through the valley of darkness, for he is truly his brother's keeper and the finder of lost children. And I will strike down upon thee with great vengeance and furious anger those who attempt to poison and destroy my brothers. And you will know my name is the Lord when I lay my vengeance upon thee."	j. JULES: E allora ascolta questo passo che conosco a memoria, è perfetto per l'occasione. Ezechiele, 25:17. "Il cammino dell'uomo timorato è minacciato da ogni parte dalle iniquità degli esseri egoisti e dalla tirannia degli uomini malvagi. Benedetto sia colui che nel nome della carità e della buona volontà conduce i deboli attraverso la valle delle tenebre, perché egli è in verità il pastore di suo fratello e il ricercatore dei figli smarriti, e la mia giustizia calerà sopra di loro con grandissima vendetta e furiosissimo sdegno su coloro che si proveranno ad ammorbare e infine a distruggere i miei fratelli, e tu saprai che il mio nome è quello del Signore quando farò calare la mia vendetta sopra di te".

Figure 3b

REFERENCES

A Fish Called Wanda. Dir. Charles Crichton. Metro-Goldwyn-Mayer. 1988.

Ascheid, Antje. "Speaking Tongues: Voice Dubbing in the Cinema as Cultural Ventriloquism." *Velvet Light Trap* 40, 1997. 32-41.

Bechelloni, Giovanni. "Televisione e Nazionalizzazione degli Italiani," *La Chioma della Vittoria: Scritti sull'Identità degli Italiani dall'Unità alla Seconda Repubblica*. Ed. Sergio Bertelli. Florence: Ponte alle Grazie, 1997. 415-42.

Benjamin, Walter. "The Translator's Task." *The Translation Studies Reader*. Ed. Lawrence Venuti. London-New York: Routledge, 2012. 75-82.

Citizen Kane. Dir. Orson Welles. RKO Radio Pictures. 1941.

Don Camillo. Dir. Julien Duvivier. Produzione Film Giuseppe Amato. 1952.

Diadori, Pierangela. "Doppiaggio, sottotitoli e fenomeni di code-switching e code-mixing: la traduzione dei testi mistilingui." *Italica*, 80.4, 2003. 531-541.

Father of the Bride. Dir. Vincente Minnelli. Metro-Goldwyn-Mayer. 1950.

Ferrari, Chiara. *Since When is Fran Drescher Jewish? Dubbing Stereotypes in* The Nanny, *and* The Sopranos. University of Texas Press. 2010.

Game of Thrones. Home Box Office, 2011.

The Godfather. Dir. Francis Ford Coppola. Paramount Pictures. 1972.

Gone with the Wind. Dir. Victor Fleming. Selznick International Pictures. 1930.

Hatim, Basil and Mason, Ian. *Discourse and the Translator*. London: Longman, 1990.

Inglorious Basterds. Dir. Quentin Tarantino. Universal Pictures. 2009.

The Lord of the Rings: The Fellowship of the Ring. Dir. Peter Jackson. New Line Cinema. 2001.

Newmark, Peter. *A Text Book of Translation*. New York: Prentice-Hall International, 1988.

Nuovo cinema paradiso. Dir. Giuseppe Tornatore. Cristaldifilm. 1988.

Paolinelli, Mario and Di Fortunato, Eleonora. *Tradurre per il doppiaggio: la trasposizione linguistica dell'audiovisivo: teoria e pratica di un'arte imperfetta*. Milan: Hoepli, 2005.

Pulp Fiction. Quentin Tarantino. Miramax. 1994.

Raging Bull. Dir. Martin Scorsese. Chartoff-Winkler Productions. 1980.

Sapino, Paola. *Portrait of a lady (1908) di Henry James e la trasposizione cinematografica (1996) di Jane Campion: testo letterario, testo filmico e doppiaggio*. Finale Ligure: Tipografia Bolla, 2000.

The Big Lebowski. Dir. Joel Coen, Ethan Coen. Polygram Filmed Entertainment. 1998.

The Big Trail. Dir. Roul Walsh. Fox Film Corporation. 1930.

The Devil's Holiday. Dir. Edmund Goulding. Paramount Pictures. 1930.

The Searchers. Dir. John Ford. C. V. Whitney Pictures. 1956.

The Simpsons. Dir. James L. Brooks, Matt Groening, Sam Simon. Gracie Film. 1988.

Il Sorpasso. Dir. Dino Risi. Incei Film. 1962.

Star Wars: Episode V – The Empire Strikes Back. Dir. George Lucas. Lucasfilm. 1977.

To Kill A Mockingbird. Dir. Robert Mulligan. Universal International Pictures.1962.

La Vacanza del diavolo. Dir. Jack Salvatori. Paramount Pictures. 1931.

Venuti, Lawrence. *The Scandals of Translation: Towards an Ethics of Difference*. London-New York: Routledge, 2002.

Vincendeau, Ginette. "Hollywood Babel: The Multiple Language Version." *Screen*, 29.2, 1988. 24-39.

La vita è bella. Dir. Roberto Benigni. Melampo Cinematografica. 1997.

Whitman-Linsen, Candace. *Through the Dubbing Glass: The Synchronization of American Motion Pictures into German, French and Spanish*. Frankfurt am Main: Peter Lang GmbH, 1992.

The Wizard of Oz. Dir. Victor Fleming. Metro-Goldwyn-Mayer. 1939.

Why Could *La Tata* Only Be Italian American?
Analyzing the Cultural Complexity Behind the Italian Dubbing Adaptation of *The Nanny*

Eleonora Buonocore

It is a well-known fact that the main character of *The Nanny*, Francine Fine, interpreted by the proudly Jewish actress Fran Drescher, is a Jewish character, yet the Italian adaptation of the show carries no trace of her Jewish heritage. On the contrary, Francine Fine becomes Francesca Cacace, an Italian American immigrant in New York, and the Italian dubbing transforms most of the show's references to Jewish culture into references to Italian culture in an impressive display of cultural superimposition. What is most extraordinary about this cultural operation, though, is how pervasive it was, and how successful it was, so much that it led to a generation of Italians who genuinely believed that the original *"nanny"* simply was Italian American. Starting from said premises, this study seeks to understand the circumstances that rendered this process of cultural super-imposition possible. In short, why was this adaptation so successful despite it being a total distortion of the original series? What specific aspects of the cultural background of the nanny made Francine Fine so apt to be transformed into an Italian American? Could this adaptational strategy work just as well for any other ethnic group?

The complexity of the relationship between the American TV show *The Nanny* and its Italian adaptation, *La tata* is unique to say the least. There is little scholarship on the Italian adaptation of *The Nanny*: the most important essay on this topic is the third chapter in a volume by Chiara Francesca Ferrari.[1] The chapter in question, entitled "Dubbing Yiddish, Hidden Rabbi: *The Nanny* in Translation," (Ferrari 2010: 52-71) was the first scholarly essay to confront this particular notion of cultural adaptation though dubbing, analyzing the process through which *La tata* transformed a Jewish American nanny, "the flashy girl from Flushing" into "an Italian American whose family comes from Frosinone" (2010: 52). Its analysis focuses on the issue of translating American television abroad, and especially on how 90's TV shows (specifically, *The Nanny*, *The Simpsons* and *The Sopranos*) portrayed ethnical differences using mainly stereotypes. In this framework, *La tata* is just one example of how a stereotype (that of a young, uncultured, low class Jewish woman) can be adapted in different ways depending on the country that 'receives' the adaptation. Ferrari's essay provides important insights into the process of adaptation that transformed *The Nanny* into *La tata*. She remarks that other countries tried to adapt the format of *The Nanny* to their own culture, but mostly by remaking completely their show for each respective culture, as happened in Poland, Russia, Greece, and in the Spanish version for the Latin American market. Moreover, she observes that *La tata* follows a unique format which she defines as "the middle ground between a more traditional translation and a complete remake" (2010: 53). This extensive adaptation process takes place only through dubbing, as "the Italian version changes significantly in setting and introduces local elements in the dialogue, employing exclusively Italian voiceover actors" (2010: 53).

---

[1] To date, the only work of critical literature entirely devoted to the Italian adaptation by dubbing of the TV Show *The Nanny* is the book by Chiara Francesca Ferrari (2010) *Since When Is Fran Drescher Jewish*, which echoes even in the title the surprise that any Italian viewer would have in discovering the Jewish heritage of Fran Drescher, *The Nanny*.

While Ferrari's insight remains invaluable for a study of *The Nanny*, there is still much ground to be covered regarding this rather unique case of adaptation carried out through dubbing alone. The reason why this process of cultural rewriting (using only the dialogue) was possible lies in the common space that lower class Jewish American and Italian American immigrants inhabited in New York. This essay will show that the character of Francine Fine is born out of this specific New York city context, in which a kind of Jewish character such as Francine Fine could develop. I refer here specifically to a lower-class New York environment in which Jewish families lived side by side with other immigrant families, especially Italian American families.

This context created a unique blend of immigrant cultures which already had grown accustomed to each other, as can be seen by the many subtle changes made to the respective traditional cultures, since these communities learned to cohabit a communal space, in which their children attended the same neighborhood schools, became friends and often intermarried.[2] Therefore, the Italian cultural adaptation that remodels a Jewish-American nanny into an Italian-American (and thus Catholic) *tata* could only work because the show takes place in New York and because of the specificity of New York's multicultural experience, which had already 'toned down' the differences so to speak, and provided a common platform for the dubbing team to engage.

In order to show the basis for the success of the Italian adaptation of *The Nanny*, one must begin by analyzing how the patterns of Jewish and Italian immigration to New York created this common ground, which is also characterized by specific class and wealth differences that shaped both the urban

---

[2] This process has been analyzed by scholars such as Diner (2001), whose insightful book provided the initial idea for this paper.

environment and its recreation in pop-culture, specifically in films and TV shows. Secondly, it is necessary to explore the influence of Italian film culture on the American collective imagination, with specific reference to how Italian movie stars with a very clear *physique du role* (such as Gina Lollobrigida or Sophia Loren) could have functioned as a model for Fran Drescher's character in *The Nanny* and thus rendered her transformation in Francesca Cacace much smoother and more believable.

Finally, it will help to examine the importance of dubbing in this process of cultural transformation, which has already been discussed by scholars focusing on modern media, but with a specific eye to how it was even possible to superimpose Italian American culture on top of the Jewish American layers in the dialogue. This process will unfold through a close analysis of a few chosen scenes taken from significant episodes, including the first and third episodes of the series, which establish the setting, and some key episodes which delve into Fran's Jewish roots, as well as others that could provide a motive to justify Francesca's Italian American heritage in the Italian adaptation of the show.

1. CROSSING PATTERNS OF JEWISH AND ITALIAN IMMIGRATION IN NEW YORK CITY

New York is quintessentially a city of immigrants, and thus it has been used as a case study for the coexistence of different social and ethnic groups since its foundation. As part of this history of immigration, the past one hundred and fifty years stand out for the sheer amount and variety of groups who have called New York their home. Recently immigration historians and Jewish historians have begun to pay attention to a special instance of coexistence between Italian American and Jewish

American groups in New York.[3] This topic is particularly complex since the label of Jewish American includes an array of immigrant groups which entered New York at different times, and with different social statuses, depending on the specific places of origin of the Jewish population (i.e. German Jews, Russian Jews etc). Yet in general, despite the obvious differences, scholars have found evidence of good neighboring relationships between Italians and Jews. This pattern can be observed starting before WWI, when, for example, we see that Jews and Italian workers shared a common interest in the labor movement. The relationship between the two groups was generally very positive, as scholar Rudolf Glanz points out "Tension and working conflict between Jews and Italians existed in very few cases" (1971: 9). They normally tended to get along so well that Gil Ribak remarks: "Scholars have repeated the praise for Jewish-Italian solidarity, asserting that Jewish-Italian relations in the labor movement were 'the most harmonious historic relationship ever to exist' between ethnic groups in America" (2014: 104). Moreover, in addition to good industrial relationships, "interethnic friction tended to soften somewhat" and "in some cases it would lead to fruitful cooperation" (Ribak 2014: 114). This relatively good disposition among Jews and Italians continued even when the two groups began to live side by side, in the same neighborhoods of New York, as Glanz notes: "During the last two decades of the 19th century, the Italians' and the Eastern European Jews' growth began to concentrate differently, often in bordering streets in New York" (Glanz 1971: 60).

This proximity between Jewish Americans and Italian Americans inevitably led to a sharing of common trades, such as the garment industry, in which Italian American women

---

[3] For a similar approach to this coexistence, interpreted as an intermixing of pathways and applied specifically to food culture, see Diner (2001).

tended to work together and sometime tried to replace Jewish women as cheaper labor. As Katie Friedman-Kasaba states: "Until the turn of the century when legislation on tenement manufacture, mechanization, and competition with lower-paid Italian women diminished their job prospects, Russian-Jewish wives participated widely in waged homework" (1996: 125).

Russian-Jewish women and Italian women in New York city largely shared a space, be that a geographical space, as in Brooklyn or in Queens, neighborhoods like Flushing, or an eco-nomical space, such as the garment industry. These co-ethnic neighborhoods also show another common trait between Jew-ish Americans and Italian Americans in New York that allows us to understand the substratum that makes Fran the nanny possible: that of a lower class, the working class of Francine Fine or of Francesca Cacace, distinctly detached from the WASP (White-Anglo-Saxon-Protestant) higher part of the city, the Manhattan of the very British Maxwell Sheffield.

This common denominator in lower-class New York united for a time both Jews and Italian Americans, and it emerges both from the show and from Fran Drescher's own biography. In fact, it was so common for Jewish kids and Italian American kids to attend the same neighborhood schools that Fran Drescher was a classmate of the famous Italian American showman Ray Romano, who became famous for a show en-tirely dedicated to the portrayal of Italian Americans in New York, *Everybody Loves Raymond*. This real-life friendship be-tween Drescher and Romano was made apparent in *The Nanny*, when Ray Romano was featured in the fifth season's episode entitled "The Reunion Show" (1998) in the role of Ray Barone, a classmate of Fran, (basically playing himself, as we will see later).[4]

The presence of Italian Americans in the original US version of *The Nanny* is substantial and important from the very beginning. As a matter of fact, in the opening episode of *The Nanny*, Fran's initial boyfriend and employer, who so unceremoniously proceeds to dump her and fire her so that the plotline of the show could begin to take shape, is called Danny Imperiali, a name that signals an Italian American origin. Moreover, one of the show's main characters is Val (Valerie) Torello, Fran's best friend and (initially) co-worker at a bridal shop. As her name clearly points to, Val is of Italian origins, and she functions in the show as an "unluckier" alter-ego for Fran. She is lower class like Fran, as uneducated as Fran, and as unsuccessful in love as Fran. She sometimes has sparks of intelligence, and sometimes even attracts the interest of men, but all in all she is a lesser version of Fran. In the final episode, she also gets proposed to by a "good man," a pharmacist, Fred, and together they move to California with the Sheffields. Such a parallel character to Fran shows how the protagonist of the show lives in an environment saturated with Italian Americans: they are her former fiancée, her best friend, her former classmates.

The existence of many Italian American characters in the original show at the same time proves the pervasive interconnection between ethnic groups in New York by the 90's, and provides a platform in which the Italian adaptation of *The Nanny*, as it transforms Francine into Francesca, not only becomes possible but also makes perfect sense. The original nanny could easily have been Italian American. Francine Fine is a lower class, uneducated Jewish woman from Flushing,

---

[4] Gliatto (October 14, 1996): "While a student at Hillcrest High (where The Nanny's Fran Drescher was a classmate), he performed in a comedy troupe at church."

mostly because Fran Drescher was herself Jewish and insisted on portraying a character of her own ethnic origin. She wanted to create the first portrayal of an openly Jewish leading female character on an American TV show, and was willing to take the risks that came with this choice (Ferrari 2010: 59).[5] Yet, the story of Francine has nothing so stereotypically Jewish that marks her apart from the story of Francesca, as the Italian adaptation shows, since it is able to superimpose an Italian American identity over the original Jewish American identity only by means of dubbing. The dialogues are the only thing that changes to morph *The Nanny* into *La tata*. It seems impossible that such a cultural operation would make sense, let alone be successful, yet it worked wonderfully. While one of the reasons for this success can be found in the underlying commonality between the parallel conditions of lower-class women in New York, the other lies in the common denominator that links the stereotypes concerning Jewish and Italian American women, specifically the stereotype of the Jewish Mother (or the Italian Mother) and of the Jewish Princess (or the Italian Diva).

2. ITALIAN AND JEWISH MODELS AND STEREOTYPES: MOTHERS, PRINCESSES, AND DIVAS

It is a common trope that Jewish mothers and Italian mothers are strong-willed women, who unify their families and function as the keeper of the culture, controlling the food production and intake of the family, and keeping a close eye on their offspring by demanding constant communication. In both these regards the image of the typical Jewish mother and that of the typical Italian mamma intersect so perfectly that they even have similar books dedicated to studying these stereotypes. An historical monograph surveying Jewish mo-

---

[5] Ferrari explicitly deals with Fran Drescher's bold choice of maintaining the Jewishness of *The Nanny*. I will analyze this point in more detail shortly.

therhood such as *You Never Call! You Never Write. A History of the Jewish Mother* and, on the Italian American front, a book explaining Italian American stereotypes on mothers such as *The Portable Italian Mamma: Guilt, Pasta, and When Are You Giving Me Grandchildren?* attest to the common ground that connects Italian and Jewish adult women in the American collective imaginary (Antler 2007; Mosiello 2010). Francine Fine's mother in the show, Sylvia Fine, a character inspired by Fran Drescher's mother, is such a quintessentially Jewish mother that she has an entire chapter devoted to her in *You Never Call!*, becoming one instance of how "television ridicules the Jewish mother, stripping her of her humanity" (Antler 2007: 187).[6] One example of the way in which Sylvia Fine becomes the butt of the jokes in many episodes of *The Nanny* concerns her attitude towards food in particular, as she is always worried about lack of food, and eating. As Joyce Antler comments, "the running joke is that this Jewish mother stuffs herself rather than her child" (2007: 184). In the Italian adaptation of the show, Francesca's own mother is still in Italy, and Sylvia Fine's character becomes Fran's aunt, Zia Assunta Iannaccone in Cacace, the wife of her father's brother. While this transformation could at a first glance look like a watering down of the relationship between the two characters, in reality Zia Assunta is the perfect Italian American mother, maybe even more so because she is an "adoptive" mother. She worries constantly about food and about Fran's love life, which, according to Mosiello are the two most distinctive traits of Italian American mothers. Francesca herself in her role as the nanny, embodies some features of the "modern Italian American mother," described as "fit, hip and stylish" much like the

---

[6] Antler (2007: 186) also defines Sylvia Fine as the quintessential Jewish mother "with her excess, whining and guilt tripping, the Nanny's mother, Sylvia Fine (Renee Taylor), embodied the image of the stereotypical Jewish mother."

Italian American TV show character Carmela Soprano (Mosi-ello 2010: 20-21).

Moreover, Fran Drescher's entire physical appearance, from her height to her long black unruly hair, and her sexy curves marks her clearly as a "Mediterranean beauty," a model of woman that could be easily recognizable by the Italian public. This model of beauty had entered the American imaginary in the 50's and 60's when Italian female stereotypes had been exported abroad through Italian cinema, becoming famous together with Italian films, from Neo-Realism to Italian comedy. This Italian dark-haired beauty, the model of an Italian Diva, had been heralded by Anna Magnani's Pina in Rossellini's *Rome Open City* (1945) but was later popularized by Gina Lollobrigida and Sophia Loren's many roles. Read through these lenses, Fran Drescher's own characterization of Francine Fine seems to have been influenced by the model of a sexy, larger-than-life, yet down to earth woman popularized in the 60's by Sophia Loren, when she won the Academy Award for Best Actress for her role as Cesira in Vittorio De Sica's 1960 film *La Cio-ciara*, which was translated into English as *Two Women*. *La Cio-ciara*, which can be better translated as "the woman from Cio-ciaria" was originally a novel by the Italian Jewish writer Alberto Moravia, before becoming an incredibly popular film, winning Loren 22 international awards, including Cannes.[7] *Two Women* was distributed in North America by Levine, and enjoyed a vast success, beloved by critics and by the public.

Therefore, it is likely that when the Italian dubbing team made the choice to transform *The Nanny* into *La tata*, and hence the Jewish American Francine into the Italian American Fran-

---

[7] Kozma-Southall (1984: 217) analyzes the sense of doom in Moravia's novel as almost a "first born offering" that the mother has to make to atone for her (and Italy's) sin of indifference. Antonucci Bisello, (2003: 45-59) explores the changes from the book to the film adaptation, especially regarding the interactions between mother and daughter.

cesca, Sophia Loren's role as a woman from Ciociaria could have influenced the choice to make Francesca Cacace an immigrant from Ciociaria.[8] *Two Women* made it possible for Ciociaria to become a well-known place to the American audience as a point of origin from which a lower class, empoverished Italian immigrant might come from. The Italian female model of "Mediterranean beauty" of course applies to any Southern Italian woman, and of course Naples and Sicily also come to mind as noteworthy places of origin for Italian Americans in film, including Loren herself in many of her Neapolitan roles, such a Filumena Marturano in De Sica's *Marriage Italian Style* (which also garnered Loren an Academy Award nomination for Best Actress).[9] In fact, Francesca's aunt, Zia Assunta Iannaccone, and her side of the family does come from near Naples, as she often likes to mention Posillipo. It is an interesting cultural operation, almost a closing of the (hermeneutic) circle, in which the stereotypes about Italians that helped shape the American imagination of Italy come back full-circle to be used in order to adapt an American TV show for an Italian audience.[10] Yet *La tata* does not erase all traces of Fran's original Jewishness. In fact, one main character remains Jewish even in the Italian adaptation of the show: Fran's grandmother, Yetta, becomes in the Italian version another aunt, Zia Yetta, Zia Assunta's sister-in-law. Yetta's Jewishness, maintained even in the Italian adaptation, is another mark of the close-knit rela-

---

[8] Carman (2014: 322-335) notes how Sophia Loren's beauty became the model for the exotic "other" woman after the success of *La Ciociara*.

[9] Ferrari (2010: 95) describes the Italian conscious attempt to control which sort of beauty was identified as Italian, which in the 90's spurred a debate, in which one side "championed Sophia Loren and Gina Lollobrigida as true Mediterranean beauties who could legitimately represent Italy and Italian women around the world."

[10] The Italian film critic Spinazzola (1985: 176-189) refers to a "filone napoletano" or a Neapolitan formula for Italian Cinema. For a modern different view of Naples in contemporary Italian films see Gaudiosi (2014: 280), who also deals with the previous filmic ways of "imagining Napoli."

tionship between Jewish Americans and Italian Americans in New York, thus rendering it possible to justify many of the Jewish elements still visually present in the show, which could not be erased merely through dubbing.

This closeness between two immigrant groups in New York, which borders on interchangeability, was not lost on the producers of the show from its inception, as Ferrari also points out when talking about "the initial distrust and uneasiness shown by CBS itself at the news that the main character of *The Nanny* would be an 'overtly Jewish' woman." Citing Cembalest's account of an encounter between Fran Drescher and some CBS executives, it becomes clear that they believed in the possibility of portraying the nanny as an Italian American, to the point of openly suggesting that "she'd be safer playing Italian" (Ferrari 2010: 59, note 12). While Ferrari uses this quote to highlight how an Italian ethnicity would be considered "safer" than a Jewish characterization, it is interesting to note that from the point of view of the storytelling and the specific 'needs' of the plot, it would be make little to no difference for a show based in New York if the nanny were Jewish or Italian, so much so that it is plausible to 'swap' one ethnicity for another. This swapping is exactly the kind of cultural operation that the Italian adaptation of the show proposes through the means of dubbing, as one can observe through a close analysis of some crucial scenes taken from a selection of meaningful episodes of the show.

3. TRANSITIONING FROM *THE NANNY* TO *LA TATA*

The first episode begins *in medias res*, inside the bridal shop owned by Fran's Italian American fiancé, Danny Imperiali, and in both the original and the Italian version, Fran is busy trying to sell a wedding dress to an already pregnant girl, assisted by her Italian American friend, Val Toriello (Lalla in the Italian version). As these details show, very little is needed in terms of adaptation in order to make Fran Italian American in this scene. It is sufficient to remove Fran Drescher's signature voice and accent, translate the dialogue fairly faithfully, and let the public believe what they want. The stage is easily set for the rest of the adaptation to take place.

The first explicit reference to Fran's Jewishness/Italian-ness coincides with the misunderstanding of the reason why Francesca showed up at the door of the family that will later employ her. First and foremost, in the Italian adaptation her name, Francesca Cacace, unmistakably betrays her Italian roots. Secondly, the translation completely excises any reference to Boca, a known location for Jewish retirees, or to Yiddish slang, such as the word "tchatchkas" for knick-knacks.[11] Instead, the writers interweave all sorts of small references to Italian places and habits, from the "tchatchkas" that become "the things that your grandmother left you" to the Italian lipstick, "il Rossetto italiano" and especially the Italian references on Francesca's resume among which the "Regina madre di Roccacannuccia," which substitutes for the queen mother, or her mother from Queens. Here, the joke was predicated on describing her own mother as being originally from a well-known nearby place, Queens. The Italian version instead trans-

---

[11] The definition of the Yiddish word "tchatchkas" comes from the article by Michael originally appeared on dailywritigtips.com, see https://www.dailywriting-tips.com/the-yiddish-handbook-40-words-you-should-know/ accessed on March 21, 2018.

forms this joke into a play on words surrounding her mother's name, Regina, and the fact that she is still in Italy, in the proverbial imaginary, far-away, and backwater town known as Roccacannuccia.[12] Moreover, we find more explicit allusions to the nanny's background when Mr. Sheffield is basically forced to hire Fran due to the agency's failure to provide a nanny in a timely fashion. As he asks her for her experience with children, Miss Fine in the original answers that she has "practically raised her sister's two kids when she was suing her chiropodist," in a self-deprecating humor that alludes to the fact that lower-class Jewish ladies tend to have gross and weird ailments. She then adds that she is from Flushing, thus "there is nothing that those kids could throw at me that I have not seen before, except possibly their trust funds." In the Italian version, this moment becomes another opportunity for a declaration of her Italian American-ness. She has practically raised the four children of her sister when she ran away with a dentist from Tivoli, and she was living in Brooklyn, with 11 cousins, so the Sheffield's children cannot pose a challenge to her. The writers used the stereotypes about Italian Americans, the large families, in order to make Fran's character more believable, and they switched New York's boroughs, from Flushing (in Queens) to Brooklyn, in order to make the setting more familiar to the general Italian public who is less than familiar with the various parts of New York City. Yet what emerges from these exchanges are the similarities, Fran Fine and Francesca Cacace are both lower class, both are poor and uneducated, and have never seen up close the kind of money that the Sheffield's kids are accustomed to having at their disposal.

---

12 The definition of the Italian usage of "Roccaccannuccia" comes from the "Dizionario Italiano Olivetti" online, https://www.dizionario-italiano.it/dizionario-italiano.php?lemma=ROCCACANNUCCIA100 accessed March 21, 2018.

The unifying character between Fran Fine and Francesca Cacace lies in their common lower-class origin. They both represent the dream of a poor girl that gets to marry the millionaire due to her good inner qualities as well as her beauty; a notion alluded to from the first episode of the show, when we discover that Francesca already knew of the poor widower Maxwell Sheffield from reading the list of Esquire's "New York's Ten Most Eligible Widowers." If Fran Fine has often been described as an instantiation of the stereotype of the Jewish American Princess (JAP), it's important to note that she is very special kind of JAP. She is more of a Cinderella than a princess in her own right. Fran is born poor, without any of the privileges of money and education that are currently associated with the idea of a JAP. Instead, a true JAP would normally have attended the best private schools, and would never need to work as a nanny for a living.

By contrast the stereotype of the Cinderella-like princess allows the Italian public to relate better to Francesca Cacace, the poor but beautiful Italian American girl who is full of life, as this is a role that the public would be very familiar with from Italian films such as *Poveri ma belli, Pane, amore e fantasia,* or *It all started in Naples*. In this sense, even Fran Fine's use of Yiddish words, which in the original function as a marker of her otherness, of her being different, in the Italian adaptation becomes an occasion to qualify such otherness as a difference in education by way of the dubbing process. In fact, the Yiddish words are dubbed with a lower-class form of Romanesque dialect that makes Francesca both more sympathetic and more reminiscent of Sophia Loren's *La Ciociara*. This can be seen as early as the first episode, when the Sheffield family joins together for breakfast, and talks about the catering for the upcoming party that night. Initially the Italian follows the English step-by-step, as Fran explains that she has a sister who is a caterer and basically offers her services for the up-coming soiree, but Maxwell promptly refuses as he says that C.C. is in charge of organizing the evening. This is when the two version begin to differ, despite using the same footage. The point of contention in both versions becomes how to give meaning to words, how to define them. When Fran, still sit-ting and eating, asks "what is a C.C.?", as if asking for the def-inition of a term, Maggie replies that she is her father's "lady friend," which he immediately corrects as "business associ-ate." Then Fran rises from the table and while pouring herself more tea, she comments "I just hope there is enough food. You know shiksas are notorious for not ordering enough food." In response to this declaration, Maxwell asks "shiksa, is that like a tchatchka?" Putting together the Yiddish word that Fran had used earlier to describe knick-knacks, with a new Yiddish word used by the nanny which generally de-scribes "a non-Jewish woman, all too often used derogato-rily," (often a blond girl without brains).[13] This exchange owes its humor to the association between words themselves and their meaning. First Fran defines C.C. as a "shiksa," and then Maxwell connects the two Yiddish words as if they were the same thing, thus associating non-Jewish women with dec-orative little objects. This entire interaction would have had no meaning in 90s Italy, since almost no one in the public would have been aware of the nuances of Jewish American culture. Therefore, the translators made an interesting choice, not only to translate Yiddish with Genzanese (a dialect from the hills outside of Rome), but also to make the whole inter-action more explicitly about the negotiation of meaning. First Francesca mistakes C.C. for a man, then upon knowing that

---

[13] The definition of the Yiddish word "shiksa" comes from the article by Michael on dailywritigtips.com quoted above, https://www.dailywritingtips.com/the-yiddish-handbook-40-words-you-should-know/ accessed on March 21, 2018.

C.C. is Max's "socia in affari" she rises from the table saying "se è in affari è una paraventa che ci guadagna sopra e a tavola le pietanze saranno un po' scarse." Literally, the Italian dubbing says "if she is in business she is a 'paraventa' that will try to make money off it and the food on the table will be meager." To this Maxwell responds by asking openly for the meaning of the unfamiliar word: "paraventa... è un termine che non ho sentito mai" ("paraventa... it's a word I have never heard"). Francesca simply explains the meaning of the arcane dialectical word, which would be hard to understand even for the Italian public. "Capisco, vuol dire furba in affari e a letto" ("I understand, it means smart in business and in bed"). Basically, she is adapting the definition of "paraventa" as taken from the *Dizionario del Dialetto di Genzano di Roma* "paravèntu 1) sm.: persona furba, astuta. Anche f.: paraventa (euf. di *paraculu*)" which literally means a cunning, astute person.[14] Here the comic effect is more direct, less subtle, yet not less effective, as Francesca describes C.C. as cunning both in business and in bed. The subsequent cut leads to a change in scene, which brings us to the shop in which Fran used to work, where the nanny has brought the kids to pick clothes for the party. In both the American and the Italian version Fran talks to her best friend, the Italian American Val/ Lalla, and she encourages Maggie to valorize her beauty. What is interesting to note here is that nothing needs to change between the two versions in order to make Francesca's Italian origins plausible: in short, the Italian heritage of the *tata* is completely plausible, nothing in her story sounds forced, at least in the first episode.

---

[14] The definition of "paraventa" is taken from Mirco e Alessandro Gallenzi, *Dizionario del dialetto di Genzano di Roma*, London, Alma Books, 2014. On-line version available at http://mgallenzi.wixsite.com/ilgenzanese/lettera-p accessed on March 22, 2018.

Moreover, Fran's use of language creates a "linguistic sep-
aration among characters both culturally and ethically" as
was already noted by Ferrari, who quotes Barbara Wilinsky
(1996) in her essay on *The Nanny* as a representation of a Jewish woman on American TV (Ferrari 2010: 64-65, note 19). Ferrari uses this citation to show how Fran's use of Yiddish em-
phasizes rather than diffuses the anxiety over her ethnicity,
yet, it's also worth highlighting how Wilinsky aptly recog-
nizes Fran's working-class background, which is one of the
core common traits shared by both Fran Fine in the American
original and Francesca Cacace in the Italian adaptation.

The attention to appearance and clothing is another common trait which brings together the stereotypical Jewish and
Italian American lower-class woman, both colorful, flamboy-
ant and vibrant, as one can also clearly observe in the third
episode of the first season, which in English is aptly titled "My
Fair Nanny," with an explicit allusion to the *My Fair Lady*.
There is a double entendre at play here: on the one hand, the
nanny is compared to the cockney girl in Cukor's film (1964),
whose accent and manners need to be elevated in order to become a true lady, but on the other hand she is also the person
who brings life, color and style to the Sheffield family and in
particular to the eldest daughter, Maggie. In the Italian version, this wordplay would not have worked, and the reference to the famous film would not have been grasped by the
public, hence the episode carries the explanatory title "Il ballo
della debutante" ("The Debutante's Ball").

The episode begins with C.C. Babcock arriving during
breakfast to announce that she has contrived to have Maggie
Sheffield invited to the biggest social event of the season, the
debutante ball.[15] The opening scenes do not present many

---

[15] The class differences are heightened in this episode, due to the dichotomy between C.C Babcock and Fran Drescher. As already pointed out by Wilinsky (1996:

significant changes between the original and the Italian version, nor do we find Fran's Jewish American identity in the foreground.

What emerges clearly though, is her poor and unsophisticated New York background. When Fran teaches Maggie how to navigate the complicated waters of the social relationships in high-school, she talks about her own experience and she does not specifically refer to her Jewishness as particularly challenging, but rather she recalls growing up poor in Queens, specifically "the cosmetology club in Flushing Queens." Instead, in the Italian version she specifically mentions first her education in Italy and then in the USA, "Le ho conosciute alle magistrali in Italia e al corso di venditori qui a New York" ("I met them at a high school for future teachers in Italy, and later at a course for vendors here in New York"). Later, as Francesca organizes a tea-party for the girls before the ball, C.C. warns her about style. The original version does not point to Fran's Jewishness, she simply talks about "her sweet 16 at Benny's Clam bar" which wasn't even the highlight of the "Flushing season." Astoria and Flushing in Queens become the markers of Fran's diversity, a diversity indicated by class and wealth, not so much by her ethnicity. The Italian dubbing again makes a point to emphasize Fran's Italian-ness "Ah quante belle feste a Fiuggi, in Italia, all'hotel Impero." Literally it says: "Oh how many beautiful parties in Fiuggi in Italy, at the Hotel Impero."

Right after this exchange, everyone is worried about how Fran would fare around the New York's "society matrons." The original and the Italian go hand in hand, until the moment when Fran enters, and she worries about mortifying Maggie at the party like her mother did when she showed up at her school dressed inappropriately. Again, in the original

---

311), while examining the American original *The Nanny*, C.C. Babckock is "the program's representative of American WASP culture."

there is no specific mention of Fran's Jewishness, just that she had a socially awkward and poorly dressed mother, who could just as well have been Italian American, while the Italian edition underlines Fran's Italian origins, and her time in school in Frosinone.[16] She then asks them to teach her how to "fit in" which in Italian gets translated as "fare le cose giuste" ("to do the right things") in order not to embarrass Maggie, and she declares that she is an "empty canvas, a blank slate" and that she is ready to become a perfect snob. The characters then rehash some very famous scenes from *My Fair Lady* when Niles and Maxwell teach her how to speak with a 'perfect' accent, or when they teach Fran table manners, or how to practice walking with her head held up by using a book.

They try to teach Fran how to pronounce the letter "r" and when she accuses them of not using it either they joke that they don't need to since they are Englishmen and they can "say anything [...they...] like and people think it is Shakespeare." In Italian, the adaptation reverses the problem with the accents: in order to signify a snobbish accent, they proceed to teach Fran how to speak with a 'fake r,' the famous "r moscia"[17] that in Italy became a sign of high-class status after it was popularized by the Agnelli family. The only explicit mention of Fran's Jewishness in this episode comes from her use of Yiddish during the first boring part of the tea-party, when Fran uses the word "shmooze," for "to chat, make small talk," which in Italian can be easily dubbed away with a more functional "scusate care, ritorno subito," ("sorry dears, I will be right back"). Moreover, when Maggie cries that this is the

---

16 In the Italian episode Francesca says: "Quando a quell'età a Frosinone mia madre per festeggiarmi all'improvviso è venuta a scuola truccata da Pierrot ma con la minigonna," which can be literally translated as "when at that age in Frosinone my mother in order to celebrate me came to my school all of a sudden dressed like a Pierrot but with a miniskirt."

17 The so-called "r moscia" is, in fact, a French or Swiss-French sounding 'r.'

worst party she has ever attended, Fran remarks that she never went to "her cousin Ira's bris." Now in the Italian dubbing the bris disappears, mostly because not many people would have been familiar with that ceremony, and it is replaced with "le feste di mio zio Andrea a Ceccano," ("my uncle Andrea's parties in Ceccano"), swapping a religious party for a secular one, and making it possible to insert another direct allusion to Italy.

In the end, the party would have been a complete flop if not for the moment in which Francesca, listening to Maggie's advice, decides to be herself. She changes into a red blazer, lets her hair flow down and engages in a sparkling if slightly inappropriate conversation with the WASP lady whose relatives came to America on the Mayflower. In the Italian version, the two ladies bond talking about Italy, where it emerges that the lady has seen "Roma e Firenze" but Francesca has only been around her native Frosinone. The lady also loves garlic, and therefore Francesca invites her to an "all Ciociara" dinner. When their new friendship leads Mrs. Wentworth to invest in Maxwell's new musical, Maxwell has to agree that Francesca's style is a winner. In the end, Fran's fresh and personal style triumphs over the stilted attitude of C.C., and Maggie learns from the nanny how to be a woman in society.

There are other episodes in which Fran's Jewishness is understated, such as the 18th episode of the third season, titled "Val's Boyfriend," in which Fran's Italian American best friend Val (in the Italian version Lalla) finds a boyfriend, while Maxwell fires C.C. The Italian title, "Bruttina ma tanto cretina" ("Ugly But So Stupid"), plays on the running joke of the episode that conflates Lalla and C.C., both deemed ugly and stupid. Throughout the entire episode the substitution between Fran's Jewish American and Italian American heritage is done perfectly. As Fran tells the tales of her family, going into disgustingly private details, the show touches on the common stereotypes that both Jewish and Italian families are very close and have a tendency to overshare personal details (especially about illnesses). In the Italian version, Fran reminds the public of her Italian origins once, while reminiscing about her time in high school in Frosinone, when she needed a new dog to keep her company, thus unflatteringly comparing her best friend to a dog. That comparison is exactly the same in English, and the joke is made even better by the director of the show, who places C.C.'s entrance immediately after the utterance "a new dog," thus broadening the equation dog = Val/Lalla = C.C. Even the scenes with C.C. at the Sushi place are perfect, as it makes sense for an authentic Italian American not to be familiar with Sushi or Wasabi.

The only moment in which an element gets lost in translation is when Fran is able to find a perfect doppelgänger for Beo Hamlish, the New York-born Jewish American composer and producer that C.C. uses to make Maxwell jealous enough to re-hire her, only because he is part of the Jewish American community, (in fact he was her music teacher). In the Italian version, though, the double becomes a "cousin of uncle Antonio" thus again reinforcing the idea that the Jewish and the Italian American community were closely connected.

Substituting the Jewish ethnic origin with the Italian does become more difficult as the show progresses and as Fran's Jewishness becomes more and more overt, as Ferrari has rightly noted (2010: 68-70).[18] Yet, even in those "more openly Jewish" episodes, some sort of verisimilitude can be maintained due to the interrelations between Italians and Jews in NYC. To give a specific example, in Season Three, episode 24, "The Cantor Show," is translated in Italian with the funny

---

[18] Ferrari also analyzes the episode "the Cantor Show" as well as the episodes that deal with Fran and Maxwell's wedding.

explanatory reference "L'unto del signore... si può smacchiare," ("the Anointed One ... can be cleansed"). In the Italian version, what makes the entire thinly veiled fiction of the episode possible is exactly the close connection between the Italian American and the Jewish communities in New York. It is not unheard of for an Italian American family to attend a function in a synagogue, since they have Jewish American relatives, such as aunt Yetta and her side of the family, in the show. In fact, in this episode we find that Fran and her mother show up at a synagogue – along with the Sheffield girls, thus it does not seem out of place that Francesca and her aunt Assunta would be there. In addition, the fact that Francesca appears from the very first moment to be interested in the physical appearance of the cantor helps justify her presence in the temple, providing the perfect excuse, which is actually the true reason why the Jewish 'version' of Fran's suddenly expresses an interest in spirituality, namely to be introduced to a good looking eligible bachelor, (in this case, the cantor).

The translators clearly had a harder time maintaining Fran's Italian American adaptation in this episode, and some of their choices definitely feel forced, yet despite this fact the episode still makes sense in Italian. The two problems that the dubbing team faced were first to explain the overabundance of Jewish religious practices to an Italian audience who is not very familiar with Jewish rituals, and only secondly to justify Fran's presence at a synagogue and her familiarity with the community at temple. Thus, the very first scenes are used to solve both problems. First, the Italian translators tried to reduce the direct references to Jewish lore as much as they could, as one can observe when they gloss over Sylvia Fine's retort to being shushed during the singing of the Shema prayer: "Calm down it's in Hebrew, what, you are afraid you are going to miss something?". This utterance was replaced with the more neutral: "Stia zitta lei, abbia pazienza, non lo vede che qui stiamo parlando?" ("Be quiet, Ma'am, can't you see we are talking here?"). Moreover, in the original language track Maggie asks if they are going to eat Chinese food after temple, in a joke that alludes to the longstanding contemporary Jewish American tradition of eating Chinese food on Christmas day. There was simply no way that a direct translation of her words would make any sense for an Italian in the mid 90's, and therefore the translators completely rewrote the sentence, so the joke would be that Maggie expects to find a "bar" in the temple, to which Fran replies explaining that it is a "church," suggesting to the viewers that a Jewish temple is like a Catholic church.

It is at this point that (in the original edition) Sylvia Fine brings forth a hilarious ham sandwich, in a self-deprecating joke, namely that a Jewish mother would bring a ham sandwich to Schul.[19] Once again, the original joke would have been totally lost on the Italian audience, and instead the dubbing allows the Italian American aunt to simply provide food for the girl, which is totally in character for her. In the Italian she warns Maggie: "va fuori, gli ebrei non lo mangiano il maiale" ("go outside, Jews do not eat pork"), thus explaining why it would be problematic to have said sandwich in the synagogue. In a sense, the Italian version is less funny but more credible: after all, what kind of Jewish mother would actually bring ham to temple? But it is perfectly credible than an Italian American guest might do so when visiting a synagogue. The translators explain Fran's connection to the Temple in the following scene, where in the original American version, Fran declares that she "had been temple shopping" and then Sylvia

---

19 "Schul" is the Yiddish word for synagogue.

gets into a shouting match with another lady at the temple, Sara, over Fran's age.

In the Italian version on the other hand, when Assunta goes to the cantor he feels the need to describe her praises as "Christian" (literally, "le tue lodi cristiane"), and when he meets Francesca he explains that he knows her because of her Jewish cousin Susan, to which Francesca replies "forse quando zia Assunta ha prestato la casa a Susan per una vostra cerimonia" and then proceeds to use the noun "circonvenzione," instead of "circoncisione."[20] This mix-up sets the stage for the fight between Assunta and the other lady, who corrects her and explains the meaning of the cloth worn by the male adult participants, which had been referred to as an "asciugamano" (a towel), which is revealed to be the holy "tallit," (the prayer shawl), to which Assunta replies that "she does not ask her guests the name of their towels." The scene is still funny, yet the humor is radically different, and this time the entire exchange does sound less credible than it had in the original.

The episode continues with Fran trying to seduce the cantor, who is himself trying to leave the temple in order to make a career on Broadway. The dubbed version tries to maintain the fiction by showing how Francesca confuses the concepts of a synagogue and a mosque, and defines the temple as a "Hebrew church," while also remarking during the party that Assunta throws for the cantor that Francesca is Christian, and that they are of different religions. The Italian episode stretches the veil of fiction that masks Fran's original Jewishness in this instance, especially when Assunta declares that she is afraid of "the Hebrew God" and of the "evil eye," which

---

[20] Literally, it means "maybe when aunt Assunta had lent her house to Susan for a ceremony of yours." And later she is trying to talk about a bris ceremony, which in Italian should be referred to as "circoncisione," but carelessly messes it up with "circonvenzione," which means "circumvention" and has nothing to do with the context. All the translations from the Italian dialogue on the show are mine.

becomes the Neapolitan "malocchio." In addition, she is quite embarrassed because she is afraid of losing her vacation spot, given that "Susan has a Jewish husband and a villa in Florida." The invention of cousin Susan, together with the reality of interfaith marriage and the ecumenical ending, in which Francesca and Assunta pray in the temple to the God of all three monotheistic religions "Dio mio e anche Dio degli Ebrei e dei Mussulmani" ("My God and also God of the Jews and the Muslims"), allows the dubbing to provide a possible if not completely plausible explanation even for one of *The Nanny*'s most 'heavily Jewish' episodes.

In contrast, it is easier for the dubbers to bring out the Italian American character of Francesca in other episodes, such as Season five, episode 18, entitled "The Reunion Show" in English. Francesca and Maxwell have recently become engaged to be married, and finally Francesca has a real reason to go to her high school reunion: to brag about her new fiancée to the same people who used to make hers and Val's life hell as teenagers. It is interesting to note that in the Italian version the title changes to "Divergenze Matrimoniali" ("Matrimonial Differences"), and the mention of the high school reunion disappears in the background, becoming a more anonymous "festa degli ex di Brooklyn" ("a party for old boyfriends from Brooklyn"), in order to avoid the problem posed by the fact that Francesca was supposedly in Italy for most of her high school education. What is interesting to note is that most of Fran's former high school classmates, as well as her friends from Brooklyn, are of Italian American descent, which in turn reinforces the adaptation's fiction that Francesca could herself be Italian American.

The Italian dubbing does not linger on the problem of justifying the apparent contradiction of how Fran could have had both an American and an Italian high-school experience, "le magistrali," as she had referred to in season one. It allows the spectators to make up their own rationalization for this anachronism, perhaps that Francesca had spent some of her high school years in Italy and the rest in NYC. More likely, the Italian translators were banking on the fact that the general public would not connect the dots between season one and season five, and tried instead to focus their attention on the guest star of the episode, Ray Barone. In fact, when the opening titles end, we find Lalla and Francesca alone at the party, eating finger foods and simulating Maxwell's presence, when they immediately meet Raymond Barone, the famous showman of the series, *Everybody Loves Raymond*. While Lalla tells the truth about Francesca's engagement, which is not believed due to the implausible yet accurate excuse she gives for Maxwell's absence (a meeting with the President of the United States), Francesca makes the inevitable meta-theatrical, cross-over joke that all the girls liked Raymond in the old times, "noi lo adoravamo tutte Raymond," which in English echoes the title of his own TV series, because "everybody loves Raymond."

To conclude, this essay analyzes how, solely through the means of dubbing, the Italian version of *The Nanny* manages to create an entirely new identity for its main character, transforming her from the low-class Jewish American Francine Fine from Flushing, Queens to the low-class Italian American Francesca Cacace from Ciociaria (and then Brooklyn). Such a successful process of cultural adaptation was only possible because of the multicultural environment of New York City, and especially due to patterns of immigration which had created a shared platform between Jewish American and Italian American immigrants. The true common denominators between Francine and Francesca are their lower-class upbringing, their zest for life, their colorful use of language. In New York city, all these characteristics can be plausibly attributed to both Jewish American and Italian American immigrants. Despite the difficulties in addressing the most explicit visual attributes of Fran's Jewishness, such as her going to synagogue, the show manages to keep up the fiction of her being an Italian American (and thus a Christian Catholic) due to the connections that were already found in the community: blood ties formed through intermarriage, friendships formed by attending the same schools, and work-related relationships created simply by sharing the same lower-class neighborhoods. All these factors contributed to the great success of *La tata* in its Italian adaptation, since they created and sustained an additional veil of fiction which made Francesca Cacace, as an Italian American nanny in New York, sympathetic, credible, and even plausible for an Italian audience in mid 90's Italy.

REFERENCES

Antler, Joyce. *You Never Call! You Never Write!: A History of the Jewish Mother*. Oxford: Oxford University Press, 2007.

Antonucci, Daniela Bisello. "Da Moravia a De Sica: La storia di una madre e di una figlia." *Nemla Italian Studies*, 27-28, 2003. 45-59.

Cembalest, Robin. "Big Hair, Short Skirts – and High Culture." *Forward*, February 14, 1997.

La Ciociara. Dir. Vittorio De Sica. Compagnia Cinematografica Champion. 1960.

Diner, Hasia R. *Hungering for America: Italian, Irish, and Jewish Foodways in the Age of Migration*. Cambridge, MA: Harvard University Press, 2001.

Emily S. Carman "Mapping the Body: Female Film Stars and the Reconstruction of Postwar Italian National Identity." *Quarterly Review of Film and Video*, 31, 4, 2014. 322-335.

Everybody Loves Raymond. Talk Productions. 1996.

Ferrari, Chiara Francesca. *Since When Is Fran Drescher Jewish?: Dubbing Stereotypes in the Nanny, the Simpsons, and the Sopranos*. Austin: University of Texas Press, 2010.

Friedman-Kasaba, Kathie. *Memories of Migration: Gender, Ethnicity, and Work in the Lives of Jewish and Italian Women in New York, 1870-1924.* Albany: State University of New York Press, 1996.

Gaudiosi, Massimiliano. "Imagining Naples: Reconfiguration of a City in the Movies by Terry Gilliam, John Turturro and Jonathan Demme." *Journal of Italian Cinema & Media Studies*, Vol. II, no. 2, 2014. 279-292.

Glanz, Rudolf. *Jew and Italian: Historic Group Relations and the New Immigration (1881–1924).* New York: Shulsinger Bros, 1971.

Gliatto, Tom. "Home Truths." *People.* (October 14, 1996), www.people.com/archive/home-truths-vol-46-no-16/

Kozma-Southall, Jan. "Omen and Image: Presage and Sacrifice in Moravia's *La ciociara*." *Italica,* 61, 3, 1984. 207-219.

Marriage Italian Style. Dir. Vittorio De Sica. Compagnia Cinematografica Champions. 1964

My Fair Lady. Dir. George Cukor. Warner Bros. 1964.

Mosiello, Laura. *The Portable Italian Mamma: Guilt, Pasta, and When Are You Giving Me Grandchildren?* Cincinnati: F+W Media, 2010.

The Nanny. CBS. 1993.

Ribak, Gil. *Gentile New York: The Images of Non-Jews among Jewish Immigrants,* New Brunswick, NJ: Rutgers University Press, 2014.

Spinazzola, Vittorio. *Cinema e pubblico. Lo spettacolo filmico in Italia: 1945–1965.* Milano: Bompiani,1985.

Wilinsky, Barbara. "'Who Talks Like That?' Foregrounding Stereotypes on *The Nanny*." *Mediated Women: Representation in Popular Culture.* Ed. Marian Meyers. Cresskill, N.J.: Hampton Press, 1996. 305-320.

Filmic Transmission of American Culture 'Before Its Time'
The Italian Dubbing Of Zemeckis' *Back To The Future*
(A Case Study)

Philip Balma & Giovanni Spani

Starring Michael J. Fox as "Marty McFly" and Christopher Lloyd as "Dr. Emmett Brown" (a.k.a. "Doc."), Robert Zemeckis' Sci-Fi Blockbuster *Back to the Future* was one of the most successful and most talked-about films of the year 1985, both in the United States and abroad.[1] Zemeckis was fortunate enough to win an Oscar for Best Original Screenplay (shared with Bob Gale) in 1986, yet little to nothing has been written about the significant difficulties and unavoidable challenges encountered by those dubbing artists whose efforts made this motion picture available and accessible to non-Anglophone audiences.[2] Released in early July of 1985 in the US, the film was first projected in theaters for Italian audiences on October 18th of the same year.[3] In other words, the artists who voiced the characters for the Italian version of the language track had approximately three months of time to render one of the most iconic films of 1980s cinema for Italophone audiences who had no real knowledge of American life in the 1950s, and whose vision of life in the United States in the mid '80s was almost entirely shaped by US-

---

[1] See: "I film più visti in settimana - Il futuro soprattutto." *La Stampa*, Oct. 26, 1985: 18. For information on the film's box office earnings, see also: https://www.the-numbers.com/movie/Back-to-the-Future#tab=summary.

[2] Christopher Lloyd's character "Doc" was voiced by the most recognizable dubbing artist of the 20th century in Italy, the late Ferruccio Amendola.

[3] See: "Prime visioni a Roma." *L'Unità*, Oct. 18, 1985: 20.

produced films, television shows, music, and a number of other products (clothes, beverages, candy, etc.) sold internationally.

Although the first words uttered by Marty's character in *BttF* are deliberately casual (and, hence, less than memorable), it's interesting to note that he uses a very internationally-recognizable American expression the first time his speech is not accurately reflected in the words pronounced by his 'Italian counterpart' Teo Bellia (the artist who lent his voice to Marty's character in Italy). In fact, in the now-famous scene where Marty plugs his electric guitar into a humongous amplifier (which explodes as soon as he strums his guitar with vigor), young McFly's stunned remark after being blown a number of feet backwards is simply "Rock 'n' roll," (04:42), though in the version entitled *Ritorno al futuro* (*Return to the Future*) he exclaims "Super stereo!"[4] instead. While, ironically, the Italian release of the film uses two English words in this case which happen to be of common use all over Europe, one should also bear in mind that Marty's use of the words "Rock 'n' roll" on this occasion is not a reference to his preference for a particular kind of music, but rather, his slang-ish way of expressing how shocked and impressed he was at the power of the amplifier he accidentally destroyed. In other words, Marty's utterance could have been left 'as is,' so to speak, and simply recorded/repeated with an Italian accent, but the effect of such a stylistic choice would have taken something away from the quality of the dubbing. Very few Italians, in fact, would have reacted to the explosion of an amplifier by saying "rock 'n' roll," both now *and* in 1985, so the words

---

[4] Although a rather accurate transcription of the Italian dialogues for *Back to the Future* (*BttF*), known as *Ritorno al futuro* (*RaF*), does exist on the world wide web (http://www.geocities.ws/anjaqantina/backtothefuture1.html), for the purpose of this study all utterances in Italian were transcribed from an Italophone copy of the film.

"super stereo" are an imperfect, yet completely acceptable and reasonable solution adopted in the process of translating and dubbing this film.

In *BttF* Marty's girlfriend is a secondary character played by actress Claudia Wells. In the role of "Jennifer Parker" she only appears in a few sequences in the opening of the film as well as the famous final scene in which Doc says the phrase "where we're going we don't need roads," (which has since been printed on thousands of T-shirts that have been sold worldwide).[5] When Marty arrives to school late, he runs into Jennifer at the main entrance, and she uses a term that is specific to American high schools and has no true linguistic counterpart in the Italian high school system of the time:[6]

> 00:06:49–"If you get caught it will be four <u>tardies</u>[7] in a row."
> **"Se ti trova sono quattro <u>note di ritardo</u> in quattro giorni."**

Although the noun "tardy" (which is derived from the word "tardiness") is almost identical in spelling to the Italian adverb "tardi" (meaning "late") and pronounced in a somewhat similar fashion; it would have made little sense to 'make up' a false, yet catchy figure of speech simply for the purpose of dubbing a single film. This is the reason why *Ritorno al futuro*, for lack of a better word, actually *coins* the expression "note di ritardo," (*tardiness notes*) to explain away the small pieces of paper that Marty and Jennifer's principal will soon hand them when he catches them sneaking in to

---

[5] In fact, they are still for sale online.

[6] The authors of this essay both attended public schools in Italy in the 1980s and early 1990s.

[7] When the word "tardy" is used as a noun, to indicate a form of admonishment or punishment students would receive for entering school late, the rare plural form "tardies" is called for when there are multiple instances of tardiness. See: https://www.merriam-webster.com/dictionary/tardy.

school late, after the first bell had rang. In actuality, most Italian high school students in the 1980s would not have been allowed to walk into class (or school) late, after their first class of the day had already started. In fact, based on how Italian public schools functioned at the time, they would have been far more likely to wait until the end of their first lesson and attempt to enter then, (a practice that students under 18 could not engage in without needing their parents to sign an official booklet either before or after the fact).[8] When principal Strickland (whose name clearly recalls the word "strict") catches Marty and Jennifer sneaking through the halls, he is quick to remind our male lead that he's been late four times in a row. Unfortunately, and rather unprofessionally, he also takes the time to speak ill of the young man's father:

> 00:07:40
> "You remind me of your father when he went here, he was a slacker too."
> **"Mi ricordi tuo padre quand'era qui, anche lui era un buonanulla."**

According to the web-based version of the *Garzanti* Italian-English/English-Italian dictionary, the best translation of the word slacker would have been the word "fannullone," (i.e.: idler; loafer; sluggard; slacker),[9] yet the insult "buonanulla" used in this case–which corresponds to the English expression "good-for-nothing"–comes close enough to rendering the originally intended meaning without impeding comprehension or altering the plot or tone of the film in any way.

---

[8] In central Italy, this practice was simply known as "entrare alla seconda ora," or rather, "entering at the second hour (of class)."
[9] See: https://www.garzantilinguistica.it/ricerca/?q=fannullóne.

Without a doubt, the hardest cultural references to translate in *BttF* concern the conversation between Marty and the owner/manager of a diner (in 1955). The dubbers' attempt to translate culturally and chronologically specific information and figures of speech used by Marty (whose vocabulary reflects American suburban life in 1985), and to employ said material to create confusion and ambiguity between two individuals in another language (*any* language), was simply and inevitably destined to fail.

> 00:37:38
> [Owner of the diner [O] speaking to M]
> "Hey, kid, what'd you do, <u>jump ship</u>[10]? What's with the life preserver?"
> **"Ehi, che ti è successo, ragazzo? <u>Ti si è affondata la nave</u>? Perché porti il giubbotto di salvataggio?"**
>
> 00:38:24
> [M speaking to O]
> "Give me a <u>*Tab*</u>."
> **"Dammi una <u>Fanta</u>."**
>
> 00:38:27
> [O speaking to M]
> "I can't give you a <u>*tab*</u> unless you order something."
> **"Fanta che? Vuoi della fantascienza da bere?"**

---

[10] The idiomatic expression to "jump ship," employed in this scene has two specific meanings: 1. "to leave the company of a ship without authority" 2. "to desert a cause or party especially abruptly" (see: https://www.merriam-webster.com/ dictionary/jump%20ship). Since the former is intended here, in light of the fact that Marty's vest is misidentified as a life preserver, the Italian-dubbed version of the film hinted that his ship *must have sank,* as if only a member of the US Navy or an individual employed at sea would ever don a vest like his. In modern Italian, the expression "abbandonare la nave" (lit. *to abandon ship*) could have been used to render only one of the aforementioned meanings (the latter), so even though the Italophone language track for Zemeckis' motion picture clearly misses the subtlety of the naval vocabulary being uttered, it does at least clarify and contextualize the kind of misunderstanding that has taken place.

Although the word "tab" (spelled with a lowercase 'T') can be used in American English to mean "bill" or "check;" which gives birth to the humorous wordplay in this scene, Marty's character had actually tried to order a soda called "Tab" (stylized as TaB), a Coca Cola product which (unbeknownst to him) was not released until 1963 (Walker 2005). The lesser-known soda called Tab was never popular in Italy and has never been available for sale on a noticeable scale, so it makes perfect sense that any references to it were excised before the feature was considered ready for Italian distribution.

The Italophone language track in this case shows that the dubbing artists chose to forego the impossible task of creating a play on words involving the name of a popular soda and a common word for "check," opting instead to have Marty order a *Fanta*, a soda that is very popular in Europe but would have been virtually unknown in America in 1955. Since the original play on words is literally impossible to reproduce in this case ("I can't give you a _tab_ unless you order something"), the version released in Italy associated the brand-name "Fanta" with the Italian word for Science Fiction (fantascienza), giving birth to an extremely implausible exchange, regardless of the context or chronology of the plot. More than any other segment of the film, however, it is the following exchange that presented the likes of Teo Bellia (the actor who dubbed Marty's voice) with an impossible conundrum:

00:38:29
[M speaking to O]
"All right, give me a *Pepsi Free*."
"Dammi una *Pepsi Senza*."

00:38:32
[O speaking to M]
"You want a <u>Pepsi</u>, pal, you're gonna pay for it."
"Se vuoi dire <u>senza pagare</u> hai sbagliato porto."

Unfortunately for Bellia, Pepsi had released a brand of caffeine-free cola in 1982 that became very popular with the name *Pepsi Free*. This enabled the Anglophone screenwriters to lean on one of the more commonly accepted meanings of the adjective *free* (i.e.: free of charge, at no cost) in crafting yet another chronologically-specific reference that was intended to create confusion between Marty and the owner of the diner. Since *Pepsi Free* was not available in Italy in 1985 when *BttF* was released, there was no direct cultural correspondence that one could hope to utilize in the translation process.

The awkward reference in Italian to a (non-existent) drink called *Pepsi Senza* (*Pepsi Without*), which was necessary to set up the utterance "senza pagare" (*without paying*), represents both a potential failure on the part of the Italian dubbing team[11] as well as another example of a concept that may very well be impossible to render satisfactorily in Italian translation. It's interesting to note that in this case the Italophone version hints back to Marty being mistaken for a sailor when he is told "hai sbagliato porto," or rather: "you've chosen the wrong port" if you think you can order something without paying. Only seconds after the young version of Biff enters the diner and begins to pester and bully Marty's father George, who happens to be seated right next to him. In fact, since Biff calls George by his last name,

---

[11] A dubbing team consists of the following members: dialogue writer, dubbing actor(s), dubbing director. See: Ulrych 2014.

both characters (Marty and his father) would have reason to be offended by his behavior and his choice of words.

00:38:55
[Biff speaking to George]
"Hey, I'm talking to you, McFly, you <u>Irish bug</u>."
"Ehi, sto parlando con te, McFly, <u>Irlandese del cacchio</u>."

When Biff calls George McFly an "Irish bug" he is in essence calling him crazy,[12] yet the Italian version makes no reference to George's mental state, simply referring to him as a "darned Irishman." The utterance "Irlandese del cacchio,"[13] much like the adjective darned[14] in American English, makes use of an expression that is often substituted for a more vulgar one.

During the 42nd minute of the film, Marty is shown sleeping in a dark room. Having hit his head in an unfortunate car accident, he believes he is talking to the adult version of his mother as he describes the experience of traveling back thirty years in time as a nightmare. Lea Thompson, in the role of Lorraine (but this time as a teenager), makes him aware that he is still in 1955 right before switching on the light. The main source of comedy in this scene stems from the notion that Marty's teenaged mother is *very* attracted to him. Once Marty realizes that his pants have been removed he hesitates to get out from under the covers, sitting back down and instinctually covering his midsection with a blanket. At this point Lorraine (identified as "L" in the dialogue transcribed below) and Marty engage in an awkward exchange; which is complicated by the fact that, in 1985, Calvin

---

[12] See: https://www.merriam-webster.com/dictionary/bug.
[13] See: http://www.treccani.it/vocabolario/cacchio2/.
[14] See: https://www.merriam-webster.com/dictionary/darned.

Klein was not a known brand of clothing in Italy. For this reason, perhaps quite intelligently, the dubbed version refers to "Levi Strauss" instead of "Calvin Klein," in order to draw directly from the schemata of Italian audiences, who were very much accustomed to buying Levi's jeans. In fact, in the mid 1980s Levi's jeans were probably the most popular jeans available for sale in Italy, from any country.

00:43:40
[L speaking to M]
 "I've never seen <u>purple</u> underwear before, <u>Calvin</u>."
"Non avevo mai visto mutandine <u>firmate</u>, <u>Levis</u>."

00:43:45
[M speaking to L]
"<u>Calvin</u>? Why do you keep calling me <u>Calvin</u>?"
"Levis? Ma perché continui a chiamarmi <u>Levis</u>?"

00:43:49
[L speaking to M]
"That is your name, isn't it? <u>Calvin Klein</u>? It's written all over your underwear."
"Levis è il tuo nome, no? <u>Levi Strauss</u>? Ce l'hai scritto dappertutto, anche sulle mutandine."

00:43:53
[L speaking to M]
"Oh, I guess they call you <u>Cal</u>."
"Oh, forse ti chiamano <u>Lev</u>."

00:43:47
[M speaking to L]
"No, actually, people call me Marty."
"No, veramente, mi chiamano Marty."

00:44:06
[L speaking to M]
"Pleased to meet you <u>Marty...Calvin...Klein</u>."
"Piacere di conoscerti <u>Levis...Marty...Strauss</u>."

In spite of the brilliant (and chronologically necessary) choice to substitute one brand of clothing for another, it's worth noting that in this scene the color of Marty's underwear (purple) is completely excised from the Italian translation. In all likelihood, this was done in order to render the original Anglophone utterances in a similar if not identical amount of time when recording them in Italian. Furthermore, one of the other features that has often been an indicator of the high quality of the work undertaken by the Italian film and television dubbing industry is the care these formidable and creative artists and professionals have for the correspondence between lip movements and the specific sounds being uttered by the characters on-screen.[15] For obvious reasons some compromises have to be made each and every time a film is dubbed, and some historical, political or popular culture references (including slang) are most often, if not always, going to be impossible to translate effectively. Nevertheless, the imaginative solutions employed in this scene are as noteworthy as they are successful.

When Doc realizes that the only way he might be able to send Marty back to the year 1985 is to channel a source of power equivalent to a strike of lighting, he expresses his distress with the somewhat old-fashioned usage "Great Scott!" (00:53:18).[16] The dubbed exclamation "Bontà divina" ("Di-

---

[15] Gouadec 2007, 56: "...the translated sequence has to fit both with the duration of the original speech sequence and with any visible lip movements (whenever the actor's face can be seen). This can be daunting, especially with certain languages. This technique is also referred to as 'lip synching'."
[16] See: https://www.merriam-webster.com/dictionary/Great%20Scott.

vine goodness"), is also of archaic origin. In fact, on a con-
ceptual level one could trace it all the way back to Dante
Alighieri, who is commonly recognized as the symbolic fa-
ther-figure of Italian literature as well as the father of the
Italian language, in his *Divine Comedy* (*Par.* VII, 64: "la divina
bontà"). Given the impact Dante had on the formation and
evolution of the Italian language, it should come as no surprise to see that even one of the greatest epic poems of the
Renaissance, Ludovico Ariosto's 500-year old masterpiece
Orlando Furioso, includes the very words used by Ferruccio
Amendola in lending his voice to Doc's character, in the exact same order (see: Canto XLI, Stanza LI: 4).

Approximately four minutes later Doc and Marty are inside the high school, and Lorraine makes a public display of
her physical attraction to her son when she loudly asks her
friends "Isn't he a dreamboat?"–though the Italophone version "È un amore, vero?" (which could loosely be translated
as "He's a darling, right?") uses a term that is less specific and
can be understood quite literally, as it is not slang.[17] The term
"amore," which is the standard noun for "love," is quite frequently used to describe both males and females in Italian,
though it is more typical to call a male a dreamboat in modern American English. Along similar lines, when Lorraine
tells Biff to get his "meat-hooks off" of her in the high school
cafeteria (1:00:33), the version screened in the *Bel Paese* opted
for "manacce," which is simply a pejorative form or the plural
term "mani," meaning hands. Unable to help himself from
rushing to his mother's aid, Marty comes very close to being
assaulted by Biff (who is twice his size) before Principal
Strickland intervenes and prevents them from fighting. In an
effort to present Biff's character as ignorant and unsophisti-

---

[17] See: https://www.merriam-webster.com/dictionary/dreamboat.

cated, the screenwriters made him unable to use even simple puns (as he does not understand them) in conversation. This strategy certainly adds greatly to the comedic value of the scene, given that Biff was attempting to sound bossy and emphatic while instead giving a public display of his lack of intellectual prowess. Instead of the well-known pun "Why don't you make like a tree and leave," Biff hesitates halfway through asking the question and says "…why don't you make like a tree.… *and get out of here*?" (1:01:06). If one considers the obstacles faced in dubbing this motion picture, it's worth restating the notion that in the aforementioned diner scene *no translator on earth* would have been able to find legitimately acceptable and linguistically parallel solutions. There simply was no way to properly render equivocal conversations about soda products that were unknown to the target audience of the Italian dubbers. This might explain away the choice to completely ignore Biff's embarrassing verbal *faux pas* in this scene, and to wisely opt instead for the *correct* use of the slang expression "alzare i tacchi" (*to lift one's heels*).

In a hilarious, mixed homage to the *Star Wars* and *Star Trek* franchises, Marty finds himself having to dress up like an alien from outer space in order to force his father George to ask Lorraine out to the school dance (by frightening him half to death):

1:02:43
[M speaking to G in disguise]
"My name is <u>Darth Vader</u>."
"Il mio nome è <u>Darth Vader</u>."

1:02:52
[M speaking to G in disguise]
"I am an extra-terrestrial, from the planet <u>Vulcan</u>."
"Sono un extra-terrestre, e vengo dal pianeta <u>Vulcano</u>."

Interestingly enough, both of the famous Sci-Fi universes referenced in this scene are very popular in Italy, especially the *Star Wars* films. Given the huge impact and success these films had in the United States, Marty's usage of the infamous name "Darth Vader," draws easily and directly from the schemata of most American viewers. This *could have been the case* for Italian audiences as well, but due to a rather humorous coincidence in the history of the Italian dubbing industry the clear allusion to George Lucas' lightsaber-yielding villain was potentially lost on numerous filmgoers. When the original *Star Wars* was released in Italian, the name of Darth Vader's character had actually been changed to "Lord Fener," merely in an attempt to avoid a silly phonetic association between one of the most legendary characters of film history and a toilet-bowl, which in modern Italian is called a "water," (pronounced "vater").[18] Leo Bettia, however, simply pronounced the name Darth Vader in Italian with a touch of an American accent (specifically, the vowel sounds). The result of this choice was that it became more difficult to identify the reference Marty is making for many of his fellow compatriots, yet in all fairness the inability to grasp this allusion would not have ruined the scene nor impeded comprehension, it simply would have made a funny moment in the plot a little less funny.

One of the sequences that solidifies the extremely shy, inept nature of George McFly's character has become iconic amongst die-hard Anglophone fans of *BttF* for the ridiculous and embarrassing dialogue it contains. In his efforts to coach his father before he approaches Lorraine to ask her out, Marty very smoothly suggests telling her that *destiny* had *brought* them together. George scribbles down some notes in

---

[18] On this subject, see also Felice Beneduce's essay contained in this volume.

a small pad to remember them, and then proceeds to make a fool of himself by stumbling over his own words:

> 1:04:50
> [G nervously speaking to L]
> "Lorraine, <u>my density has popped me to you</u>."
> **"Lorraine, <u>il delfino ci ha uniti</u>."**
>
> 1:05:13
> [G nervously speaking to L]
> "I'm your <u>density</u>. I mean… your <u>destiny</u>."
> **"Sono il tuo <u>delfino</u>. Cioè… il tuo <u>destino</u>."**

In the original version, George makes two confusing mistakes, switching the noun "destiny" with "density" and the verb "brought" with "popped." One of the reasons this scene works as well as it does is the rhyme pattern that exists between the words George spoke and the ones he meant to speak. Hence, the choice to 'amend' the use of "density" with the Italian word for dolphin ("delfino,") makes perfect sense, considering the need or desire to use a term that rhymed with "destino." The same creative, innovative, and often remarkably effective approach undertaken by the dubbing artists gave birth to a uniquely perfect translation eight minutes later in the film. While hatching a plan to make sure his parents end up together at the school dance, Marty has to reassure his father that he will not have to fight anyone to achieve this purpose. In the process, he accidentally calls him "Dad," then manages to improvise a plausibly playful use of language designed to distract George from picking up on his slip-up. In this particular instance, by substituting "dad" with another term of endearment used for fathers in Italy ("pa'," intended as a shortened version of "papà") the result can only be described as flawless and brilliantly conceived:

1:13:08
[M speaking to G]
"Look, you're not gonna be picking a fight, <u>Dad... dad-dad-daddy-o</u>!"
"Ma non devi fare a pugni, <u>Pà... pa-pa-ra-pa-pa-pa</u>!

Not unlike the reference to "tardies" in the first few minutes of the film, the sequence in which Marty "parks," with Lorraine before the dance employs the verb "to park" in a way that is specific to American culture. The decision to let the events of the plot clarify the use of this expression, which was translated literally with the verb "parcheggiare," makes for a slightly awkward and mildly off-putting exchange in linguistic terms,[19] yet nothing of fundamental importance is lost in this process.

1:17:46
"Marty, I'm almost eighteen. It's not like I've never <u>parked</u> before."
"Marty, scusa, ho quasi diciott'anni. Vuoi che non abbia mai <u>parcheggiato</u>?"

One of the most subtle and delicate cultural responsibilities of a dubbing artist is to have a care for how different races, ethnicities, and nationalities are represented in terms of their speech patterns. During the "Enchantment Under The Sea" dance at the high school, the film introduces viewers to a handful of secondary characters; namely, the Afri-

---

[19] See: https://www.garzantilinguistica.it/ricerca/?q=parcheggiàre.

can-American guitarist and singer Marvin Berry[20] and his fellow band-members, all of whom are of the same race. When the band takes a break, Marvin speaks into the micro-phone and says "Don't nobody go nowhere" (1:18:45). His grammatically incorrect use of a double negative (the correct usage would be "Don't anybody go anywhere") is potential-ly intended to mimic the speech patterns of his specific racial group in the context of 1950s America. It's worth noting, in fact, that the landmark supreme court ruling designed to end racial segregation in American schools (Brown v. Board of Education) only took place in 1954, one year before the chronological context of (most of) the film.[21] It follows that Zemeckis' and Gale's choice to make Marvin sound unedu-cated, or simply under-educated, has some legitimate grounding, as it indirectly reflects the long, troubled history of the American struggle to end racial inequality in our schools and beyond. The decision to avoid injecting these subtleties into the lines of dialogue uttered by the members of the band, while falling in line with an approach that shows a level of political correctness and sensitivity for the need to respect and cherish diversity in all its forms, also removes one of the cultural notions embedded in the origi-nal language track of *BttF*. In *RaF*, on the other hand, Marvin Berry's announcement that the band was going on break re-flects a level of language and diction that most adult per-formers might use in an effort to better relate to a young group of adolescent students. When Marvin says: "Nessuno si muova, ragazzi" ("Nobody move, guys"), his demeanor is warm and charismatic as the screenwriters intended, but

---

[20] For the purpose of this film, the character of Marvin Berry is supposed to be a cousin of Chuck Berry, author of the song *Johnny B. Goode* which is featured in a key scene (when Marty plays guitar on stage).
[21] On this subject, see: Chen 2018.

there is nothing that denotes a particular difference between his modes of expression and those of the middle-class, Caucasian boys and girls dancing to his music.

Not surprisingly, racial differences and racial discord, filtered through the perspective of young characters in 1955, do find their way into the plot of *BttF*: during the 81st minute of the feature Marty gets locked in the trunk of a car by three of Biff's friends, one of whom is recognizable because he wears 3D glasses everywhere he goes. As it turns out, they have locked Marty in the trunk of the band's car, and the 'break' the musicians were taking consisted of sitting in their vehicle and smoking marijuana. Once Biff's entourage slams the trunk shut with Marty inside, the owner of the vehicle steps out and protests. The (white) character identified as "3D" in the credits then uses an outdated racial epithet and rudely yells at him to mind his own business:

1:21:08
"Hey, beat it, spook, this don't concern you"
"Vattene, muso nero, non sono affari tuoi!"

One can only be impressed with the ingenuity required to take a *passé*-sounding racial slur like "spook"[22] only to translate it as "muso nero," which is both very strong ("black muzzle" or "black face") and specific without being particularly reminiscent of other insults that were considered typical and parallel in meaning in Italy in 1985. A few seconds later a *very* tall and large musician exits from the back passenger-side door. Surrounded by a cloud of thick smoke as he gets out of the car, this imposing individual is not even

---

[22] In contemporary American English, this term is now often used to refer to a spy or a secret agent, though it can also mean ghost or specter. See: https://www.merriam-webster.com/dictionary/spook.

remotely afraid of three high school students from the sub-urbs. Without hesitation, he angrily asks: "Who you calling spook, peckerwood?"–which prompted the dubbing team to make a lateral move, so to speak. Instead of trying desperately to find an Italian word that might be used to insult a white person (especially a poor white person and/or a white person from the American South),[23] they chose to call "3D" a "bed-wetter" ("piscialletto"); or rather, they used an insult that focused on his youth and lack of maturity instead of one that emphasized his skin color.

As a *coda* of sorts to this case study on the dubbing practices that gave birth to *Ritorno al futuro*, it is strangely necessary to also discuss the Italian release of another 1985 film starring Michael J. Fox, or rather, *Teen Wolf*, known in Italy with the title *Voglia di vincere* (*The Desire to Win*). *Teen Wolf* was released shortly after *BttF* in the United States, and the same could be said for its distribution in European cinemas. In Italy, after the incredible box-office success of Zemeckis' film, a rather questionable marketing campaign was enacted to convince Italian-speaking filmgoers that *Voglia di vincere* was a pseudo-sequel to its predecessor, given that the same actor starred in both films. Specifically (see image 1 below) a number of posters were printed which contained the following text: "Michael J. Fox ritorna dal futuro con una grande… VOGLIA DI VINCERE." The English equivalent of this type of bait-and-switch advertisement is "Michael J. Fox comes back from the future with a great… DESIRE TO WIN."

---

[23] See: https://www.merriam-webster.com/dictionary/peckerwood.

Figure 1 [24]

Furthermore, in an effort to solidify this ploy by means of word-of-mouth once the trailer for *Voglia di vincere* started airing on TV and in movie theaters, a decision was made to utilize the dubbing process to change the name of the main character from Scott to Marty. Even though this (possibly) unprecedented publicity scam undertaken by the Italian distributors of the film did have the effect, at least initially, of filling more seats in more cinemas, the end result made specific segments of the film confusing, while also pointlessly toying with the expectations of paying customers who have a number of motion pictures to choose from when they can make time in their busy lives to go see one.

The most noteworthy and embarrassing consequence of these dubbing practices pertains to a sequence that takes place early in the film. Marty/Scott is at a party with a bunch of his friends from high school, where many kegs of

---

[24] Visible online at the following URL address: https://www.filmtv.it/film/7852/voglia-di-vincere.

beer are made available to a crowd of underage drinkers. During the course of the party, a game called "five minutes in the closet" begins, which involves girls picking names of random guys out of a hat only to be locked in a closet with them (supposedly to make out) when their turn came up. Imagine, if you will, the following experience: the images are being projected onto a very large screen, so even though the names of these boys were written on a small piece of paper it was quite easy to read them for all members of the audience in the theater. A girl with dark, short hair draws the name "MALCOLM" from the hat, and looks disappointed when she reads it. Next to her, a girl with long, blonde hair is holding a piece of paper that clearly says "SCOTT." She also looks upset, as if she were not interested in our protagonist. The first girl notices the second one's reaction, so when her turn comes up, and no one has 'claimed' Scott yet, she simply states that his name was the one she drew from the hat. In other words, after showing a theater full of hundreds of people that the two young men who were 'up for grabs' in this game were named Malcolm and Scott, the lead female character looks at the piece of paper in her hand and states "It says Marty."

Not wanting to give too much weight to questionable (and, somewhat hilarious) practices like the ones mentioned above, this study comes to a close by reminding its readers of the grave consequences that can come to pass when the act of translation, in any context, is not taken seriously or undertaken professionally by trained experts. As Daniel Gouadec reminds us in his volume entitled *Translation as a Profession*:

> The whole point is that the slightest defect in the translation and sound track will immediately have an adverse effect on the audiences. Hence the obsessive attention of the dubbing team [...] to the slightest cultural, linguistic, and technical detail. (2007: 56)

REFERENCES

Ariosto, Ludovico. *Orlando Furioso*. Torino: Einaudi, 2015.

Back to the Future. Dir. Robert Zemekis. Universal Pictures. 1985.

"I film più visti in settimana–Il futuro soprattutto." *La Stampa*, Oct. 26, 1985.

"Prime visioni a Roma." *L'Unità*. Oct. 18, 1985.

Chen, Michelle. "Brown v. Board of Education ended school segregation. So why are schools still not integrated?" *NBCNews.Com*. May 17, 2018. https://www.nbcnews.com/think/opinion/brown-v-board-education-ended-school-segregation-so-why-are-ncna875051.

Gouadec, Daniel. *Translation as a Profession*. Amsterdam and Philadelphia: John Benjamins Publishing Company, 2007.

Teen Wolf. Dir. Rod Daniel. Wolfkill Productions. 1985.

Ulrych, Margherita. *Traces of Mediation in Rewriting and Translation*. Milano: EduCATT, 2014.

Walker, Andrea. "First there was Diet Rite, then Tab and Diet Pepsi. In 1982, Diet Coke arrived on the scene. Now, with Coke Zero, the latest entry on the market, it's a real..." *The Baltimore Sun*. Jul. 7, 2005. http://articles.baltimoresun.com/2005-07-07/business/0507070035_1_diet-soda-coca-cola-diet-rite.

"FABRIZIO, TRADUCI PER ME"
LANGUAGE, POWER AND THE OTHER IN
"MARIO PUZO'S *THE GODFATHER*"

Richard Bonanno

"Mario Puzo's *The Godfather*" by Francis Ford Coppola is a landmark production within the gangster genre and one of the defining films of a new wave of American cinema. With its innovative cinematography and exceptional cast, the film was a tremendous commercial success upon release. Nonetheless, the polished motion picture betrayed significant tension and disagreement that had been at play among staff and executives during all stages of production. In one of many artistic differences with producers of Paramount Studios, Coppola remained steadfast in his desire to create a period piece, one that would be shot on location and include detailed references to the Italian-American experience.[1] The use of extensive dialogues in Italian is but one technique aimed at enhancing the cultural and historical authenticity of the film, and this departure from Hollywood convention would have a profound effect on English-speaking moviegoers, conveying the mysteriousness of the Corleone family and the politics of power. Moreover, Coppola's insistence would yield rather felicitous results in the presentation of one of the film's central themes, Michael Corleone's fateful rise to power as leader of the Corleone crime family. An examina-

---

[1] Biskind provides a colorful account of the highly stressful and problematic making of *The Godfather*, ultimately stating, "Not only did *The Godfather* revive Paramount... it was like a jolt of electricity for the industry" (1998: 152-165).

tion of the adaptation of the novel to the screen and of the subsequent translation of the film for Italian viewers, *Il Padrino*, reveals how the form and function of language in *The Godfather* provide a key toward interpreting the charged drama of the protagonist and the world of Italian Americana to which he belongs.

Early in her affair with Michael Corleone, the young Kay Adams asks her lover how she might effectively explain their rather transgressive relationship to her parents. While observing his reflection in the mirror and carefully running a comb through his hair, the son of Don Corleone responds with peculiar irony,

> Just say that you've met a brave, handsome guy of Italian descent. Top marks at Dartmouth. Distinguished Service Cross during the war plus the Purple Heart. Honest. Hard-working. But his father is a Mafia chief who has to kill bad people, sometimes bribe high government officials and in his line of work gets shot full of holes himself. But that has nothing to do with his honest hardworking son. Do you think you can remember all that? (Puzo 2016: 113)

The amorous encounter will prove their last before Michael becomes unexpectedly embroiled in the Corleone family's criminal activity and resorts ultimately to killing bad people himself. Indeed, book I of Mario Puzo's *The Godfather* comes to a thrilling close with the brutal murders of Virgil Sollozzo and a conspiring police captain at the hands of Michael Corleone. The event would precipitate the "Five Families War of 1946" and lead to the necessary exile of the young assassin to Sicily, the land from which his father, Don Vito Corleone, had fled to save his own life some thirty years earlier. The otherwise honest and hard-working Michael would have to wait several years before seeing Kay Adams again and eventually marrying her, though under vastly different circumstances.

Having worked strategically to create and maintain the peace among the criminal organizations after his spectacular rise to power, Don Vito Corleone would have never wished for either a war or, more lamentably, the involvement of his son Michael in the family business. By the same token, Michael ostensibly would have never envisaged such a fate for himself. His act of retaliation toward those who had shot his father "full of holes" effectively seals his destiny and offers a significant amount of subtextual coloration in the novel. It is not simple revenge that motivates him: the allure of power and the allegiance to family play a role in Michael's unexpected turn of fate and feature among the principal themes in Mario Puzo's best-selling novel. The savvy reader, nevertheless, finds the most compelling drama in the heightened tension between the progressive ideals of the New World and old-world values represented by the two protagonists, a theme that Francis Ford Coppola would elevate to new heights in his adaptation of the text, and the protagonist's relationship with Kay Adams exemplifies in part this tension.

The tale of Michael Corleone's path from decorated war hero and Ivy League student to head of the most powerful crime family in the United States takes center stage in the 1972 Paramount production *The Godfather*. In the novel, Puzo depicts the Don's youngest son as deliberately aloof and pointedly more concerned with his fair-skinned companion than with the traditional festivities on his only sister's wedding day. Readers first encounter him seated with the wholesome and flowery Kay "at a table in the extreme corner of the garden to proclaim his chosen alienation from father and family" (Puzo 2016: 17). The protagonist's detachment will, of course, be short-lived. His deliberate involvement in the family business presages the axiom stated so forcefully by Puzo at the close of his monumental work of fiction, "Many young men started down a false path to their true destiny. Time and fortune usually set them straight" (Puzo 2016: 423). The sudden and unexpected transformation sets Michael Corleone's life and vocation on a course quite different from what has always been desired by both him and the family patriarch, but he will strive to mitigate the circumstances of his new role and to return to the path embodied by his love affair with Kay Adams, a predominant theme in the motion picture.[2]

The screenwriting team of Mario Puzo and Francis Ford Coppola would face a number of obstacles in their adaptation of the novel, foremost among them framing its narrative action, which is as vast as Michael Corleone's supporting cast of characters. Fraught with particular encumbrances is the realm of cinematic adaptation in which the intrinsic qualities of the print and film media seem to exponentially complicate the process and indeed make it impossible to remain faithful to the original work. Nevertheless, Puzo, the writer, and Coppola, the filmmaker, succeeded in producing a screenplay that captures the most theatrical elements of the original text. Their focus on Michael Corleone and the trajectory of his meteoric rise to power in effect disentangles his tale from several other secondary narratives and subplots in the novel, and his relationship with Kay is of fundamental importance in this light. The motion picture would enjoy extraordinary success at the box office following its release in 1972 and feature prominently in the realm of popular culture

---

[2] Thanks to the extraordinary cinematography of Gordon Willis, Michael is initially depicted basking in light. Once his transformation is complete, he, too, will be cast in a shroud of darkness.

in the United States on many levels in subsequent years,[3] offering testimony to its commercial and artistic superiority
compared to the novel from which it was adapted.

The enduring power of the motion picture is very much a
product of Coppola's personalized reading of the novel and
of his refined audio-visual conception of the film narrative,
which synthesizes the essence of Puzo's hard-boiled novel.
One might argue that the stylistically exceptional film production ultimately led Puzo to state in later years that his
only regret was not having written a better book even
though it had appeared on the *New York Times* list of best
sellers for 67 weeks and been a tremendous commercial success. (Puzo 1972: 41) Despite the supremacy of the film production, Coppola has never missed an opportunity to express his debt of gratitude to the original author of the saga;
one need only consider the precise title of the film, "Mario
Puzo's *The Godfather*," in order to better understand the extent of the director's appreciation. Of course, a director can
never remain entirely faithful to the original text from the
narrative, yet such a shortcoming may very well be for the
better.[4] Such is the case with Coppola's adaptation of the
groundbreaking crime novel from which many digressions
and indulgences were effectively eliminated. The more focused narrative and the visual vibrancy of Francis Ford
Coppola's "Mario Puzo's *The Godfather*" demonstrate that
nothing is lost, but rather much is gained in adaptation. Crit-

---

[3] The reception of Puzo's novel and the three films of the trilogy in popular
American culture has been discussed at length by scholars in the fields of cultural, literary, and film studies. Christopher Messenger's *The Godfather and American
Culture: How the Corleones Became "Our Gang"* (2002), provides a good starting
point for readers interested in this topic.
[4] Puzo's novel, despite its commercial success, was not well received by critics.
For a summary of this reception and a defense of the "deeply prophetic" power
of the novel, see Chiampi (1978: 18-31).

ics from a variety of disciplines have shared their views concerning the motion picture since its release, though not all have waxed poetic, especially in the months following its release when the novel still resonated strongly. The interpretive lens has changed over the last four and a half decades as scholars continue to be drawn to the film, which has achieved mythical status in the realm of popular culture; the novel and its adaptation appear today as little more than an afterthought. It is clear that Puzo and Coppola drew from their own experiences in order to present the story against a backdrop that has become arguably the most memorable and original — albeit highly controversial — depiction of twentieth-century Italian-American history and culture.[5]

The appeal and reception of the motion picture in Italy, where the ethnic and political roots of the story lie, are quite another story. A careful analysis of the Italian dubbed production reveals that much of what the film gains in adaptation, is lost in its subsequent translation. An Italian viewer comes away with a different impression of the central themes and a markedly deficient perception of the particular sociocultural milieu that have made the original motion picture so appealing to English-speaking audiences. Michael's suggestion to Kay in the original text concerning how she might explain to her parents their rather unorthodox love affair discloses the contextually divergent nature of his family's heritage while also setting in motion one of the central themes of

---

[5] In the wake of the publication of the novel — and to a greater degree following the release of the motion picture — this particular representation of Italianità would create some degree of stigma towards Italian Americans. As Messenger points out, "Indeed, *The Godfather's* dominion over Italian American signification in American culture gave rise to the curious fact that after 1969, to the average American popular culture consumer, Italian Americans *are* Sicilians; they are represented by Mafia Hoodlums and their enterprising murderous families to the exclusion of any other complex network of groups" (2002: 111).

the adapted work, one that will ultimately suffer in translation. Despite his patriotism, intellect and honesty, his "Italian" pedigree runs counter to the upstanding Yankee, salt-of-the-earth lineage of Kay's family and the world to which he apparently aspires. Michael Corleone's origins represent in the strictest sense an obstacle in the pursuit of legitimacy (and, by extension, the American dream in the twentieth century), and the most subtle and emblematic formulae through which this topos is presented in the original English production are not readily perceptible to the Italian viewer as a result of the somewhat problematic nature of the dubbed version.

The world of Italian Americana is surprisingly more difficult to translate to Italian audiences, and such is noticeably the case with *Il Padrino* in which the dubbing director endeavored to find an effective means of conveying the distinct linguistic and cultural identity of the Corleone family and the supporting cast of characters.[6] These men and women are well-versed in Italian, Sicilian and English, though each to varying degrees. In the American production, the members of the Corleone family and the lieutenants and soldiers of the criminal organization speak predominantly English and, at times, use a number of expressions in Italian and Sicilian that reveal their ethnic background. The colorful language, cast of characters, traditions and material culture included in the original production offer nothing short of a nostalgic tableau as recalled by both Coppola and Puzo in what one might more aptly categorize as a period piece dealing less with gangsters than with the Italian-American experience at large, and the sights and sounds of this world are as evocative to

---

[6] Two dubbed versions of *The Godfather* (*Il Padrino*) are in commerce, the more recent one produced in 2007. In this essay all dialogues are drawn from the original version, directed by Ettore Giannini and featuring Giuseppe Rinaldi, Cesare Barbetti, Ferruccio Amendola, Arturo Dominici, and others of note.

Italian Americans as they are fascinating to English-speaking viewers less familiar with the unique twentieth-century subculture. Many non-verbal elements would at times lose their significance in the dubbed version, such as "football weddings," bottles of cloudy anisette with handwritten labels, take-out Chinese dinners, and recipes for tomato sauce.[7] However, a significant challenge would be that of rendering the inflection and substance of the speech and verbal expressions, which are, for the most part, easily understood by English-speaking viewers though distinct from standard American English. Sonny Corleone's "badda bing badda boom badda bang" or "Save it for the lib'ary" would prove as difficult to communicate as Clemenza's philistine utterance of "Paulie? You won't be seeing him no more," or his melodious Italian-American line, "Hey Mikie, why don't you tell that nice girl you love 'er? (singing) I love you with all-a my heart! If I don't see you again-a soon I'm-a gonna die!"[8] These are but a few examples of speech that convincingly portrays the period and the unique cultural milieu in the motion picture yet remains imperceptible to Italian audiences. Nonetheless, the translation of this language would perhaps prove easier to the post-production staff than the task of solving a particularly thorny technical problem: the translation of Italian dialogues, above all when language is tied to Michael Corleone's "identity crisis" and is, as a consequence, symbolic in nature.[9]

---

[7] Coppola unveils many symbols, such as these, drawn from the world of Italian-Americana in his audio commentary to the film included in *The Godfather Collection*.

[8] All translations, unless otherwise noted, are the author's. For a fairly thorough script complete with production stills and extensive notes, see Jones (2007).

[9] For a general discussion of the theory and practice of film dubbing, with particular attention to the levels of translation and complications within the process, see Pavesi (2005). For a broad examination of the theory and practice of dubbing and the dubbing industry in Italy, see Paolinelli and Di Fortunato (2005).

In a departure from Puzo's text — albeit for rather obvious reasons given the director's penchant for verisimilitude
and the expressive potential of the film medium — Coppola
had chosen to include a number of dialogues in Italian that
would be accompanied by English subtitles whenever necessary for English-speaking audiences.[10] This technique was
relatively uncommon in Hollywood productions of the period. Those actors playing Italian nationals in the sequence
based in Sicily would speak Sicilian and Italian but very little, if any, English. Coppola and his casting director would
make a significant effort to cast actors who could move
seamlessly from one language to another in order to depict
the world of Italian Americana with the utmost authenticity.
In the original production, Al Pacino, Richard Castellano, Al
Lettieri, Morgana King, Lenny Montana and Tony Giorgio
are among those actors who speak both English and Italian
in New York. The most convincing Sicilian American is Al
Lettieri, whose physical presence, acting skills, and excellent
command of Sicilian, Italian and English make his performance as the villain Virgil Sollozzo truly extraordinary. The
average English-speaking viewer might find the Italian dialogues in the New York scenes particularly expressive, an
effect that will be discussed later.

Despite his surname and rather convincing southern-Ital-
ian complexion and stature, Al Pacino managed to communicate in Italian and Sicilian with some difficulty. Further
complicating matters, executives at Paramount Studios were
opposed to casting a relatively unknown actor in what would
be his first starring role, but Coppola was unwavering in his
support of Pacino "in the role that secured his stardom"

---

[10] The English production includes less standard Italian than Sicilian dialect and/
or variations of Italian with marked Sicilian and southern inflection. For the purposes herewith, Italian will include by extension Sicilian unless otherwise noted.

(Heller 2016). In the novel, Michael Corleone is described as having taken a course in Italian at Dartmouth, while the film version of the character would be familiar with Sicilian and Italian though ultimately uncomfortable speaking both. The director was well aware of the actor's inability to speak Italian, which would necessitate revision of the shooting script and some degree of improvisation on the set.[11] The director uses Pacino's linguistic deficiency to great advantage in order to advance the theme involving Michael's identity crisis; his preference for English betrays a character who, at least initially, aspires to move beyond the rather weighty familial and cultural constraints of the family business and his heritage. However, once the transformation of the character is complete, i.e. from honest and patriotic immigrant son to head of the Corleone crime family, English will become the new language of power and free enterprise of which the American-born and college-educated Michael shows a masterful command.

Pacino was not the only lesser-known professional involved in the project; Coppola himself had not gained extensive directing experience by the time he began working on the film. A refined artistic vision shines through nonetheless, specifically with regard to the screenplay and its attention to the representational nature of language. Indeed, Coppola took advantage of certain lead actors' inability to speak Italian or Sicilian, and his insistence on including authentic dialogues featuring actors proficient in the languages serves not only to heighten the authenticity but also to foster a feeling of "otherness" among those characters not belonging to the

---

[11] One such example is Michael's first meeting with Vitelli. While the shooting script had originally featured Michael as actively participating in the conversation describing Apollonia, "Coppola adjusted the scene so only the bodyguards speak" (Jones 2007: 149).

seemly impenetrable world of the Corleone family. This sentiment extends also to viewers of the film who are unfamiliar with Italian and Sicilian even though Coppola's adoption of subtitles would make them privy to the subject matter of dialogues. The inclusion of dialogues in both English and Italian has undeniably contributed to the mythic quality of the gangster archetype in *The Godfather*.

An examination of several key sequences in the light of specific industry techniques and Coppola's original intent serves to illuminate the ways in which the form and function of language are altered in the Italian production as a matter of necessity. The focus on Michael's Sicilian-American identity loses its sharpness, and the resulting tension between his particular heritage and that of the wholesome Yankee is almost non-existent.

One of the dubbing director's first technical priorities would be that of recreating the distinct socio-cultural position of the Corleone family and those members of the criminal underworld within the greater context of mid-twentieth-century American society. Language and culturally specific modes of speech feature among the more emblematic characteristics of the members of the immediate Corleone family and, by extension, the criminal organization to which they belong. It would, therefore, be necessary to create a socio-linguistic analog in the Italian production in order to denote the distinctiveness of the members of the Corleone family, who speak an Italianized version of the Sicilian dialect. Their speech, on the one hand, could be readily understood by Italian viewers and, on the other hand, would serve to convey the mysteriously insular world of Sicilian Americana. Conversely, a more refined, standard Italian would be spoken by those "others," the non-Sicilian Americans, such as Kay Adams, who do not share the seemingly impenetrable linguistic and cultural heritage of the Corleones and the old-world, criminal organization to which they belong. In the case of Kay Adams, this notion is conveyed verbally in the opening sequence as the fair-skinned, brightly dressed young American woman needs Michael to explain what is happening around her at his sister's wedding. As shall be discussed further on, the final sequence of the film will visually convey Kay's disconnection from this world. Both Michael Corleone and Tom Hagen, however, communicate in standard Italian with regularity, which demonstrates the college education of each character and Michael Corleone's rejection — at least initially — of his lineage and of the dishonest way of life of his family. While generally effective in presenting the substance of the narrative to Italian viewers, this method fails to adequately represent the exponentially more divergent worlds of Sicilian Americana and English-speaking America. Consequently, the sense of "otherness" is diminished in the Italian production as the shroud of mystery is lifted from the inhabitants of the Corleones' world.

Two scenes in the English production bring to light this notion and lend support to the assertion that Coppola deliberately has Michael stumble through his Italian and Sicilian dialogue and ultimately resort to English: the meeting with Virgil Sollozzo and Captain McCluskey in the restaurant in the Bronx and the discussion with Vitelli in front of his tavern in Sicily. In each instance, Michael commences by speaking Italian and/or Sicilian and then switches rather symbolically to communicating in English, apparently for reasons other than that of the actor himself feeling ill at ease. The translation of these scenes would pose problems, and the result alters the symbolic nature of English as the new language of power.

The aforementioned romantic interlude between Michael and Kay included in the novel serves once again as a point of reference, though this time we might more aptly refer to the corresponding scene presented in the motion picture, which depicts the young lovers saying goodbye after having dined together in Kay's hotel room. Earlier in the day Michael had planned to spend time with Kay and then travel to the hospital to visit his ailing father following the failed attempt on his life. The hotel scene marks Michael's final meeting with Kay before Captain McCluskey will literally destroy his clean and boyish looks later in the evening in the hospital sequence, the protagonist's vocational turning point. Once at the hospital, Michael realizes that something is amiss and consequently acts in a cold and cunning manner in order to preserve his father's life and uphold the supremacy of the Corleone family. After successfully repelling a group of would-be assassins, he calmly lights the cigarette of his terrified and trembling accomplice, Enzo, the baker, whom he had recruited to stand guard with him at the entrance of the hospital. Only slightly surprised at seeing the detached steadiness of his own hand in the midst of a life-threatening situation, Michael has begun to embrace *ante litteram* his destiny as member of the criminal organization that he will eventually lead. The beautifully filmed next scene depicts the bruised and jaw-broken — albeit calm and calculating — Michael in the center of the meeting room along with the interim Don, his *consigliere*, and the caporegimes.[12] As the men discuss their strategy for confronting

---

[12] Puzo goes into some detail concerning the injury to Michael's head and sinuses for which he would ultimately require surgery. The description is particularly telling in the light of Michael's identity crisis: "The distortion of the left side of his face made him more native. It was the kind of disfigurement common in Sicily because of the lack of medical care. The little injuries that cannot be patched up simply for lack of money. Many children, many men, bore disfigurements

Sollozzo, the camera zooms in slowly and with a determination similar to that with which the protagonist willfully seals his fate, revealing a man who is both physically and psychologically different from the one that was having dinner with Kay Adams in the hotel room not 24 hours earlier. Seated confidently at the very center of the administrative circle of the Corleones, Michael devises the brilliant scheme to murder Sollozzo and McCluskey.

The fateful meeting with Sollozzo and McCluskey comprises one of the most significant scenes of the film, and Coppola worked painstakingly to remain faithful to the text and create the most visually evocative and spectacular scene possible.[13] Seated with Sollozzo and McCluskey at a table in the center of the unpretentious eating establishment, Michael has come to broker a deal with Sollozzo while the police captain offers him protection. Michael sits uncomfortably in his chair with his back to the entrance while Sollozzo leans eagerly forward, assuming a position of power even though the Don is still alive and, as a result, Sollozzo's business venture remains stunted. Turning to McCluskey, Sollozzo states, "I'm gonna talk Italian to Mike," and then proceeds to address Michael in Sicilian. The waiter is able to understand them, so Sollozzo is careful to speak only after he has taken their order and walked away. McCluskey, who had given the order to remove the Don's bodyguards from the hospital, is already privy to Sollozzo's criminal activity, making it unnecessary for Sollozzo to hide the details of the conversation from him, especially when Sollozzo seems to be looking for nothing more than a truce and McCluskey

---

that in America would have been repaired by minor surgery or sophisticated medical treatments" (2016: 329-330). In the Sicily sequence Coppola depicts Michael with a handkerchief in his hand regularly wiping his nose.

[13] Coppola recounts the importance of this scene in great detail in his audio commentary included in *The Godfather Collection* (2008).

appears solely interested in the culinary experience. Moreover, in the immediate vicinity there are no patrons capable of overhearing their exchange in either English or Italian. Sollozzo's choice of addressing Michael Corleone in Sicilian implicitly demonstrates his desire to exert authority over him. Nervously mumbling a few words in response, Michael acknowledges Sollozzo's expression of regret concerning the unfortunate situation but comes to an impasse when attempting to offer a more detailed response in Sicilian. "What I want is a guarantee..." he states, reverting forcefully to English through clenched teeth, a tactic that appears to have a dual purpose. Making McCluskey privy to the conversation, Michael helps assuage any suspicion that he may have, but, more importantly, his deliberate use of English signifies his bid to reclaim the authority of the Corleone family before both the upstart *mafioso* and the police as an institution.

The scene in the English production illustrates the underlying tension between Michael's American ambitions and the old-world values typical of Don Corleone's generation. The men dine in Louis' Italian-American Restaurant, a rather emblematic cross-cultural venue that encapsulates Michael's identity crisis. It also bears mentioning that Sollozzo, who has come to broker a deal, begins his diatribe in Sicilian by criticizing Don Corleone for being too old-fashioned, "tu patri, pensa all'antica" ("Your father has old-fashioned ideas"). In the dubbed version, Sollozzo turns to McCluskey and states, "Parlo un po' di business con Mike" ("I'm going to speak a little business with Mike"). He addresses Michael in Sicilian, and Michael responds in Sicilian with noteworthy, albeit incongruous, mastery given the argument at hand. He does not appear to stumble over his words, and his abrupt use of standard Italian in order to communicate his desired outcome seems misplaced as he states forcefully, "Voglio una garanzia…" ("I want a guarantee…"). Sollozzo responds in standard Italian, which remains consistent with the prevailing linguistic analog, and from a semantic standpoint the crux of their conversation differs only slightly from the English equivalent. The dubbed version, conversely, fails to convey Coppola's clever yet subtle use of language as a means of lending greater psychological depth to the protagonist.

Much like the meeting with Sollozzo and McCluskey in Louis' Italian-American restaurant, Michael's first conversation with Vitelli offers support to the notion that his deliberate use of English exposes an identity conflict, which is conveyed inadequately in the dubbed production. The entire Sicily sequence includes only limited use of English among the principal characters. There are three such instances: an allusion to Apollonia's indifference to learning English, the bodyguard Fabrizio's beckoning American soldiers to take him to America, and, most notably, Michael Corleone's use of English to address Vitelli and, as though negotiating a business deal, request a meeting with his daughter. Regarding the first two instances, Apollonia's levity seems to bear little significance within the narrative while Fabrizio's strong desire to travel to America portends the treachery that will lead to the failed attempt on Michael's life and the sacrificial death of Apollonia.[14] Referring specifically to Michael's meeting with Vitelli, Coppola indicated that he had wanted to avoid long sequences in Italian with English subtitles in order to keep viewers engaged, but the protagonist's use of English is deliberate and revelatory from a thematic standpoint.[15]

---

[14] In the novel we learn that Fabrizio, as a reward for betraying Michael, is assisted in a move to the United States. However, he is brutally murdered in the pizza place that he runs near Buffalo, NY when Michael "sends… his regards" in order to settle all family business (Puzo 2016: 411-412).

[15] Coppola audio commentary, *The Godfather Collection* (2008).

In the English production, the scene unfolds as Michael, seated with his bodyguards at a table on the patio of Vitelli's tavern, learns that Vitelli was offended by questions concerning the identity of the beautiful young woman who had recently captured his attention. The men soon learn that she is Vitelli's daughter, and Fabrizio recommends that they leave immediately given the father's growing sense of irritation. Muttering in poorly pronounced Italian, Michael first instructs Fabrizio to call Vitelli back to the table and then orders him to translate for him, "Fabrizio, traduci per me" ("Fabrizio, translate for me"). Remaining self-assuredly seated at the table as Vitelli stands before him, Michael begins to speak English, initially offering an apology and then stating that he is "a stranger" in the country. Fabrizio serves as interpreter for Vitelli, who is surprised and asks in Sicilian, "ccu è chistu? E cche v'ole de mi' figghia?" ("Who is this guy? And what does he want from my daughter?"). With candid matter-of-factness that recalls his response to Kay as he observed his reflection in the mirror, Michael quickly reveals his true identity to Vitelli by stating that he is "an American hiding in Sicily" and that his name is "Michael Corleone." Adding a note of solemnity, he indicates that there are people "who would pay a lot of money for that information," but then his daughter "would lose a father... instead of gaining a husband." After a brief, dramatic silence, Michael continues by respectfully expressing his desire to meet the man's daughter, and Vitelli, at once aware not only of the prominence of the figure before him but of the seriousness of his intentions, invites him to his house. Michael finally stands to face Vitelli, asking him, "come si chiama vostra figghia?" ("What's your daughter's name?") "Apollonia," he replies.

The importance of Michael's conversation with Vitelli and of his subsequent marriage with Apollonia cannot be underestimated in the light of the overarching theme discussed up to now, and, once again, the hotel-room encounter with Kay Adams serves as a fitting point of reference. The earthy, olive-skinned Apollonia, whose name alone underscores the socio-political underpinnings of the cultural heritage of the Corleone family, is the consummate juxtaposition to the American-born Kay Adams. While having had to coach Kay on how to explain their relationship to her parents, Michael now resorts to traditional codes of chivalry in the courtship of his Mediterranean object of affection. The consummation of the protagonist's marriage with Apollonia and her eventual death will complete his cycle of initiation into the family business as he embraces his true destiny and identity.

Translating the conversation between Michael and Vitelli clearly posed obstacles to the dubbing director, and the result would hardly prove felicitous. In standard Italian Michael instructs Fabrizio not to translate but rather to explain that there has been a misunderstanding, "Fabrizio, spiega che c'è un equivoco" ("Fabrizio, tell him that there has been a misunderstanding"). Michael's Italian dialogue then remains for the most part semantically faithful to the original English script as he states that he did not mean to offend Vitelli and that he is a "forestiero" ("foreigner") not inclined to provoking others without good reason. He then reveals his identity and his motives not only for staying in Sicily but, in essence, for speaking so candidly with Vitelli. The consecutive translation of the conversation in English and Italian between Michael and Vitelli — with Fabrizio serving as interpreter — is not easily communicated in the dubbed production. Fabrizio, rather, elaborates on Michael's statements in what comes across as an awkward dialogue culminating in Fabrizio's overly explicit statement, "Avete sentito che ha detto? Iddu si 'a sposa!" ("Did you hear what he said? He wants to marry her!"). In the Italian production, Michael's highly nuanced declaration to Vitelli loses its potency while the dramatic pause that follows it is nothing short of misplaced. Moreover, the symbolic nature of language, crucial to understanding the figure of Michael Corleone, is absent.

Il Padrino, the Italian dubbed version of *The Godfather*, is a well-crafted production, typical of the high standards of one of Italy's most successful industries. Considerable attention was given to finding a solution to some of the problematic formal and stylistic issues discussed in this essay, and the Italian dialogues of the English version were most ably translated and consequently polished with due respect given to the original. The Italian cast, which featured several highly capable *doppiatori*, such as Giuseppe Rinaldi in the role of Don Vito Corleone and Ferruccio Amendola as Michael Corleone, managed to effectively communicate the shadowy world of the Corleones, although its presentation according to the Sicilian-versus-Italian linguistic analog conjures up many of the socio-political concerns characteristic of the modern Italian Republic. The Italian viewer does come away with a more appropriate portrait of the immigrant or, more specifically, the Sicilian experience in the United States. Some of the linguistic shortcomings in the case of *Il Padrino* are overcome in the film's brilliantly conceived closing sequence, which is presented from Kay's perspective and readily exhibits the sense of "otherness" discussed at length previously. Both Kay and viewers have learned by now that presidents and senators — those inhabitants of Kay's world — also "have men killed" just as a mafia chief would, but this is, of course, a matter of business.[16] On this day, Michael, referred to as Don Corleone by one of his capore-

---

[16] Addressing Senator Geary in *The Godfather, Part II*, Michael will state emphatically that they "are part of the same hypocrisy," *The Godfather Collection* (2008).

gimes, has finally settled all family business and finds himself in the final stages of the family's move to Las Vegas.
Kissing his hand as though he were a prince, his caporegimes pledge their loyalty to him. Kay, as other, bears wit-
ness to Michael's consolidation of authority and ascendancy
to role of supreme head of the underworld, the door of
which is literally and forcefully closed both to her and to
viewers.

REFERENCES

Biskind, Peter. *Easy Riders, Raging Bulls: How the Sex-drugs-and-rock
'n' roll Generation Saved Hollywood*. New York: Simon &
Schuster, 1998.

Chiampi, James T. "Resurrecting *The Godfather*." Melus, 5.4, (1978):
18-31.

The Godfather Collection. Dir. Francis Ford Coppola. Paramount
Home Entertainment, 2008.

Heller, Karen. "Al Pacino Was Nearly Fired from 'The Godfather.'
The Rest is History." *Washington Post*, 29 November 2016.

Jones, Jenny M. *The Annotated Godfather: The Complete Screenplay*.
New York: Black Dog & Leventhal, 2007.

Messenger, Chris. *The Godfather and American Culture: How the
Corleones Became "Our Gang."* Albany: State University of
New York Press, 2002.

Il Padrino Trilogia. Dir. Francis Ford Coppola. Master Collection,
2016.

Paolinelli, Mario and Eleonora Di Fortunato. *Tradurre per il
Doppiaggio*. Milano: Hoepli, 2005.

Pavesi, Maria. *La traduzione filmica: aspetti del parlato dall'inglese
all'italiano*. Roma: Carocci, 2005.

Puzo, Mario. *The Godfather*. New York: Berkley, 2016.

_____. *The Godfather Papers and Other Confessions*. Greenwich:
Fawcett Publications, 1972.

Translating Mel Brooks' *Blazing Saddles* for The Italian Audience

Robert Lincoln Hackett & Philip Balma

Mel Brooks is one of the few artists to have joined the elite club of EGOT winners, or those who have earned at least one Emmy, Grammy, Oscar, and Tony award. His films have grossed hundreds of millions of dollars and over his sixty plus years in the entertainment industry, he long ago became one of the most influential representatives of modern American cinematic humor. Given his extensive work in the theater, as well as his early work writing for various sketch comedy performers, it is no wonder that his films should often rely on turns of phrase, slapstick, puns, and other forms of comedy that are difficult to render through the dubbing process. In addition to his wordplay, the cultural references used in his many films often go over the heads of native English-speaking audiences, and often cause problems for the international public. Despite the inherent difficulties in translating humor from one culture to another, along with the added difficulty presented by some of Brooks' comedic features and the specific Anglo-American reality they inhabit in their original versions, his films have all been dubbed into Italian to varying degrees of success. This essay will focus primarily on the single highest grossing film directed by Brooks and will endeavor to explain why it performed so poorly at the Italian box office, while another of the director's films of the same period did comparatively quite well.

Blazing Saddles is a 1974 western movie parody that grossed 119.5 million dollars at the global box office, including more than 35 million in the USA. The film earned several Academy Award nominations and was deemed culturally important by the Library of Congress in 2006. Still, the picture faced criticism at the time of its release, both for its sketch-comedy-like plot and the abundant use of the word "nigger."[1] Despite such negative criticism (which was by no means universal), this was one of the first features to earn more than 100 million dollars and it paved the way for Mel Brooks to have much more independence in his filmmaking. Yet box office success was not to be found when it was released in Italy more than a year later, on February 27, 1975. Indeed, the majority of Italian film critics of the day "lo giudicò un filmetto grossolano"[2] (Giusti 1980: 64). This reaction is based, at least in part, on a misunderstanding and misreading of numerous utterances in the film, which in part still defines how this feature is viewed and interpreted in Italy to this day and may be traced back to unmet challenges in the translation of Brooks' style of comedy.

On the surface, *Blazing Saddles* is a slapstick, farcical film about a black sheriff whose eternal optimism and quick wit allow him to overcome all odds and beat the bad guys in the end.[3] This simplistic reading of the film highlights the sound and sight gags and the situational humor of the various episodes. While this work does contain the elements listed here, the whole story is much more profound: this is, at once, a cinema lover's homage to several staples of American West-

---

[1] It is important here to use the entirety of the word in this essay, rather than a euphemism like "the 'n' word," as what is heard in the film is the derogation "nigger," and the difficulty in translation from English to Italian is inextricably linked to the reason why said word is so difficult to hear out loud for an audience from the United States, let alone to be read in an essay.

[2] "Called it a coarse little film."

[3] With a Pirandellian chase through the lots of Paramount Pictures and Fox.

ern movies and a critique of the racism both in the society of 1970s America and in the Western film genre. No element of the film makes this more clear than the frequent use of the word "nigger," which was constantly translated in Italian with the word "*negro.*"

An audience might expect for the rough, unlettered cowboys of the film (led by Slim Pickens in a brilliant performance) to use this word to disparage black people; the setting is the American west in 1874 after all. From the opening scene, in which a group of black men are working on a railroad under the gaze of their white bosses, the role of black people in this society is made clear: instead of sending horses to save a cart from a pit of quicksand, Taggart (Pickens) says that horses are too valuable, so they should "send a couple of niggers." Two of the workers manage to save the cart but are then stuck in the quicksand themselves. Once the cart is safely out of danger, Taggart leaves the two men to their fate, commenting "that's a four-hundred-dollar cart," and hence implying that the two black lives are worth less than that. One of these railroad workers, Bart (Cleavon Little) will shortly be appointed sheriff of a little town called Rock Ridge. Upon arriving, he is met with a deafening silence, after which the chairman of the welcoming committee begins the speech that he had prepared, saying "it is my privilege to extend a laurel, and hearty[4] handshake to our new..." before looking up to see Bart with his star, and finishes his speech with a dumbfounded "...nigger." The Italian dubbing team did not choose the usage *negro* here, opting instead for "*o cacchio*" after the chairman's pause, which is (roughly) to say "oh hell." This choice drastically softens the

---

[4] It is worth noting here that Brooks' use of the homophone "hearty" for "Hardy" represents one of the many nods to the director's heroes (Laurel and Hardy, in this case) in what can be seen as a "throw-away" joke. We will come back to this point shortly.

blow of Bart's arrival, though immediately thereafter all the townspeople aim their guns at him. The ease with which all of the people in Rock Ridge use the word "nigger" is what makes it so important for the film; their racism is so deeply ingrained that this word is on everybody's lips. The scene that takes place in Rock Ridge on the morning after Bart's arrival is one of the few times that translating this word with the Italian noun *negro* actually does work. Bart says to an elderly woman in the street "Good mornin' ma'am; and isn't it a lovely morning?" To which she replies: "Up yours, nigger," before walking away. The Italian translators were both fortunate and insightful in this instance, deciding that her line should be "Vaffanculo, negro." The first word the woman utters is so unexpected for the audience, (literally "fuck you,") that the impact is exactly the same in both films, though in actuality this is the only time that "negro" consists of an accurate translation of the racial slur "nigger," in the context of how (and the spirit with which) this term is employed by Brooks.

The use of the word "negro" in Italian translations of the insult "nigger" is still problematic to this day.[5] The Italian word comes directly from the Latin word for "black" (niger/nigru[m]), as does the English word "negro." Although the use of the Italian word has slowly taken on a similar negative connotation to that which the English word holds, the cultural baggage is not the same in the two languages. Furthermore, when *Blazing Saddles* was released in Italian theaters there had been but little discussion on the connotations of

---

[5] Indeed, due to a sufficiently large amount of questions regarding the use of the Italian terms *"negro," "nero,"* and *"di colore,"* Federica Faloppa wrote a short article in 2006 for the *Accademia Della Crusca* as per the distinctions among them and which to prefer in given circumstances today. To read the full article, see: http://www.accademiadellacrusca.it/it/lingua-italiana/consulenza-linguistica/domande-risposte/nero-negro-colore Last visited on July 5, 2018.

this word. Indeed, in his descriptions of the film's plot, as well as his discussion of the cinematographic and cultural background of the film, Marco Giusti (writing in 1980) used the words "*negro*" and "*nero*" almost interchangeably – perhaps favoring "negro": "Bart, un *negro* dalla lingua sciolta...," "firmerà con noncuranza la nomina del nuovo sceriffo *negro*...," "aiutati anche dai lavoranti *negri* della ferrovia..."[6] etc... (Giusti 1980: 64-65, my italics). But why insist on this point? Specifically because this comedic film is about racism, and the use of the word "nigger" is important in order for the feature's intended message to come across. Director Mel Brooks has discussed this point at length over the years; when asked if he could get away with using this particular word in a film today, he replied:

> Never. If they did a remake of *Blazing Saddles* today, they would leave out the N-word. And then, you've got no movie. And I wouldn't have used it so much if I didn't have Richard Pryor with me on the set as one of my writers. And Cleavon Little [as Sheriff Bart] was great. Even though it was allowed, I kept asking Cleavon, 'Is that all right there? Is that too much there? Am I pushing this?' and he'd say, 'No, no, no, it's perfect there'. (Weide 2012: 36)

Without that word there is no film, according to the director. It follows that an inadequate translation of the word would prevent the film from connecting with its Italophone audience.

All of which is not to say that the translation of a single word is the only problem with the Italian version of *Blazing Saddles*, translated as *Mezzogiorno e mezzo di fuoco* (which

---

[6] "Bart, a *black man* with a silver tongue..."; "will carelessly sign the nomination of the new *black* sheriff..."; "also helped by the *black* railway workers..."

could be something along the lines of *High Noon Thirty*, in English). Returning once again to the scene in which Bart arrives in Rock Ridge, the native English-speaking audience has no trouble picking up the reference to the comic duo Laurel and Hardy, while the Italian audience misses out on it entirely (*ho l'alto privilegio di consegnare questo alloro ad un uomo di fegato*) (I am privileged to present this laurel to a man with guts). While the joke in English is neither important for the story, nor particularly humorous, Brooks' motion pictures are filled with moments of this sort and not translating them in some way is tantamount to removing the director's voice from the film. Several of these references are missing from the Italian version of the film, but more important still are those jokes that are not references to previous films or comic actors, but which tell us something about the characters, are truly funny, and are completely missing from the Italian translation. One such joke is part of an exchange between Bart and his friend from the railway, Charlie, who the audience was introduced to in the opening scene. Bart rides up to his old friend in the vestments of a local sheriff, to which Charlie shows (obvious) surprise and delight, saying "Bart, they said you was hung!", to which the sheriff replies "And they was right." Although jokes lose their humor when they are explained, this short interaction deserves a moment of attention. Charlie does not have the same expertise with the English language as Bart, and as such his grammatical error ("was hung" instead of "were hanged") is both acceptable and comprehensible to a native speaking audience. Bart, on the other hand, is an excellent wordsmith and can change linguistic registers as he pleases. His reply works both as a perfectly normal response in the register with which Charlie addresses him ("and they was right" rather than "and they were right"), but the *double-*

entendre lies in the fact that Bart understands perfectly well that "to be hung" means "to have a large penis," while a person sentenced to death by hanging would be "hanged." This joke works well in English for those who know the difference between "hung" and "hanged" and when the audience accepts the fact that Bart uses the English language precisely (as he does from the very first scene). In Italian, however, how could one render such a play on words given the disconnect between the two contexts they allude to (death by hanging vs. being a well-endowed male)? The dubbed version says: "*Ma non ti avevano impiccato?*" to which Bart replies: "*Eh, c'è mancato poco*" (Didn't they hang you? – Well, it was a close call). In this case the translators did not even attempt to retain the joke in Italian. In fact, it's quite possible that they missed it entirely, fully believing in the accuracy of their work on this scene. The dialogue discussed in this paragraph lasts roughly two seconds in the film (from 00:53:56 to 00:53:58), which helps to understand the difficulty in translating a film that is 93 minutes long and full of word play. One final very brief scene will help show, perhaps, the impossibility of translating this film into Italian.

After his difficult arrival in Rock Ridge, Bart meets his co-protagonist, the Waco Kid (played with understated perfection by Gene Wilder) in the town lock-up. The two exchange pleasantries and the sheriff recounts why a "dazzling urbanite" such as himself should be in a rustic setting like Rock Ridge. In a short flashback he explains that his family had been following a wagon train (full of white people who would not let them into the train proper) which at one point is attacked by Native Americans. The white people are all killed and then the chief and a few others approach the wagon of the child Bart and his parents. The following scene takes place in a mixture of English and Yiddish, from approximately 00:33:15:

> Chief: "Schwarzes. [One of the Native American warriors raises a tomahawk, and the chief exclaims:] No, no, zayt nisht meshuge! [Short pause before the chief yells into the air, with eyes toward the sky] Loz im geyn! [Back to Bart's family] Cop a walk, it's alright. Abi gezint! Take off! [The family leaves, after which the chief speaks to the same warrior as earlier] Hosti gezen in dayne lebn? They darker than us! Woof!"

The scene, with the pauses included, lasts roughly 30 seconds and is impossible to understand without knowing either Yiddish or, at the very least, a bit of German. The scene written entirely in English would be as follows:

> Chief: "Black people... [One of the Native American warriors raises a tomahawk, and the chief exclaims:] No, no, don't be crazy! [Short pause before the chief yells into the air, with eyes toward the sky] Let them go! [Back to Bart's family] Cop a walk, it's alright. To your health! Take off! [The family leaves, after which the chief speaks to the same warrior as earlier] Have you ever seen something like that in your life?? They darker than us! Woof!"

The Italian-dubbed version of this short exchange contains a few rather interesting choices, to be examined one at a time:

> Chief: "*Minchia*. [One of the Native American warriors raises a tomahawk, and the chief exclaims:] No, no, sono dei poveracci.! [Short pause before the chief yells into the air, with eyes toward the sky] Limonaro! [Back to Bart's family] Potete erre, niente paura. Servo vostro, eccellenza. [The family leaves, after which

the chief speaks to the same warrior as earlier] Santuzz, hai visto
che roba? Più neri di noi sono, huu!"

"*Minchia*," a stronger form of the "*o cacchio*" seen above, is
usually translated in English as "fuck" or "shit" – in any case
as a strong expletive. This is the second time in the film that
the dubbers opted not to use the word "*negri*" or "*neri*" for
what is essentially "black people." While it is true that the
chief did not say the word "nigger" as do most of the white
characters in the film[7] the chosen solution actually changes
what is seen on the screen: by saying "*minchia*" the chief is
basically suggesting that he had been unaware that they
were black before deciding to let them live. This may be the
case too in the English version, though Brooks' character
does not seem so surprised as to justify or explain away the
Italian translation in this case. Moving along to the next line
of dialogue, the chief tells his warrior that Bart's family is
made up of "poor souls." Although the information given in
the two languages is different, the notion of offering a reason
not to kill the family of African Americans (either in order
not to be crazy or because they are just poor souls) comes
across in both versions of the film. The translation of this line
is acceptable, but the next is unconscionable. "Loz im geyn"
is Yiddish for "let him (or them) go, while "*limonaro*" does
not mean "let him go" nor anything similar. In fact, neither
the *Ragazzini* 2018 dictionary nor the *Treccani* online dictionary and encyclopedia contains this word. "*Limonaro*" seems
to mean "lemon seller," and at least in the dialect of Assisi it
has been used in this way (Santucci 1966: 173-176). The most
plausible reason for the translators' choice in this particular
point in the film is that the character's lips move in a way

---

[7] And as such his role and the message thereof are written in such a way as to
underscore the differences in cultures and racial attitudes.

that is similar to *"limonaro."* The meaning behind the word has nothing to do with that which is said in Yiddish (by white-skinned actors pretending to be Native Americans); this fact leads one to believe that the translators either a) did not understand the Yiddish, which would be unacceptable, or b) decided to opt for a solution that highlights the 'demented' aspect of Brooks' humor and relies on the audience focusing on that dimension, especially given the various 'low-brow' gags present in the feature. While this might be an understandable choice for a truly difficult scene to dub, the Italian-speaking audience misses out on a fundamental aspect of the comedy of Mel Brooks, and as such it should come as no surprise that the reception in Italy of this film has a tendency toward the idea that this is nothing more than "a coarse little film" or perhaps a straight parody of the Western genre. In truth, through this roughly thirty-second exchange in two different languages, one of which is completely unexpected, Brooks brings depth to that which otherwise would be an inconsequential comedy featuring fart jokes and vulgarity.

Yet this is one of the reasons why Mel Brooks' films are so popular with native English language speakers: his (and the other writers') wit is constantly on display through densely packed lines of dialogue that can often engage viewers on several different levels. Translating *Blazing Saddles* into Italian must surely have been a monumental task, but despite some good luck (again, such as the usage "vaffanculo, negro" seen above) and a bit of inspired selections of regional accents for the various characters (Dom DeLuise with a Florentine accent works particularly well), the movie loses an exceptional amount of its original humor and gravity in the Italian translation. In contrast, Brooks' most successful film at the Italian box office, *Young Frankenstein*, does not suffer from any of these potential pitfalls.

This second motion picture to hit Italian cinemas in 1975 was written for the screen by Brooks and the protagonist, Gene Wilder, as it was adapted from an idea that Wilder had worked on years before being cast in *Blazing Saddles*. It is understandable, then, that *Young Frankenstein* should be unlike any other film that Brooks directed. Although his style of humor is evident in many parts of the screenplay (the fact that horses whinny every time that Frau Blücher's name is pronounced aloud is classic Brooksian humor), this film is not made of a series of sketches that are filled to the brim with one-liners, puns, and gags, as is common in his other works. This difference in style is a key aspect of the feature's success in the Italian language: dealing with a much smaller number of difficult plays on words to be transferred into another language, the translators were able to focus on rendering each individual joke just as well in the target language.

In the interest of claiming an inheritance from his late grandfather (the original Dr. Frankenstein), our protagonist (Wilder) travels to Transylvania. The final leg of his trip takes place on a train. This journey marks the first of two moments in which the dubbing team that transformed *Young Frankenstein* into *Frankenstein Junior* for Italian screens chose not to translate a specific portion of the original dialogue (a very brief one, in this case). A boy at a station where Dr. Frankenstein's train has stopped answers the following inquiry: "Excuse me boy, is this the Transylvania station?" (00:14:48). His reply, which leans heavily on the less-than-exceptional comedic pretense of a facile rhyme scheme, is "Ya, ya, track 29. Can I give you a shine?". Given that said rhyme scheme would have been impossible to reproduce in Italian without significantly altering the tone and content of this brief exchange, the dubbers "left it" entirely in English. Aside from the evident difficulties presented by the use of the rhyme scheme in the original language track, the reason why it was potentially considered appropriate (or at least acceptable) to leave this short conversation in English is not particularly intuitive. In a bizarre and impossible linguistic "non-place," where the exigencies of the international distribution of a movie call for it to be translated into multiple western European languages, audiences are presented with American characters who speak standard, modern, non-regional Italian, and also "foreign" characters who speak in Italian but with a German accent. In this specific, fictional cinematic context, one might assume that a famous and successful doctor, researcher and teacher would know how to speak English out of necessity, regardless of where s/he came from or what language s/he spoke in daily life.

The other (aforementioned) instance in which material from the Anglophone original version is "maintained" in the motion picture is much more climactic. It's the famous scene in which the doctor and his creature perform "Puttin' on the Ritz" for a theater full of scientists and citizens of Transylvania, that actually takes place much closer to the end of the film.

Towards the end of the 17th minute of Brooks' feature, the audience is first introduced to the character named "Inga," (Dr. Frankenstein's lab assistant played by Terri Garr) while the protagonist hops in the back of a horse-drawn cart filled with hay. Though Inga's first scene in this film is nowhere near as memorable as Igor's (the doctor's servant and gopher, played by Marty Feldman), it happens to present Italophone viewers with some of the most creative, daring, and hilariously successful work ever accomplished by an Italian dubbing team. Inga's first utterance in the original version is a singsongy invitation for Gene Wilder's character to "Roll, roll, roll in the hay..." which was modified in Italian to better match the duration of the corresponding line: "Dai, dai, fare anche tu..." ("C'mon, c'mon, you do too"). It's worth noting that, with the exception of Igor and Dr. Frankenstein, some of the comedic value of the speech patterns used by multiple characters in *Young Frankenstein* stems from the heavy Germanic accent they use (in both versions of the film, in fact, Inga speaks in this way). During their "ride in the hay" back to the castle inherited by Dr. Frankenstein, Inga hears the sound of a howling wolf and asks "Where wolf?" (00:18:26), in broken English. This question creates a play on words alluding to a werewolf, or rather, a lycanthrope. When the protagonist repeats (word for word) Inga's question to Igor, the hunchbacked servant confusedly replies "there wolf," mimicking (and perhaps mocking) the inaccurate speech patterns originally used by the young woman. Dr. Frankenstein is not clear, however, on why Igor is speaking in this fashion, as his reply sounds both like poor English and an effort to mock his interlocutor. In the Italian language track, Inga does not inquire about the location of a wolf, but rather, she says "lupo ulula" (i.e.: "wolf howls"). The verb "ulula" ends with the syllable "la," which in Italian is pronounced like the adverb "là" ("there"), to indicate a physical, geographical location. The Italophone response offered by Igor is just as bizarre, comical, and openly mocking as his original utterance ("there wolf") was, and it manages to keep the play on words (and the audience's focus) on the same parts of speech, on adverbs of place. To the statement "lupo ulula" in fact Igor answers "lupo ululà, castello ululì," transforming the verb "to howl" (ululare) into a stand-in for the adverb "lì" (also meaning "there"). In other words, although it is impossible to translate this expression literally, it consists of an ingeniously parallel play on words, hinging on the quasi-poetic repetition of similar vowel sounds (in each version) in reference to the location of a howling beast and, in a second moment, to the castle.

Approximately five minutes later into the film (00:22:15) the castle's caretaker Frau Blücher hesitates to pronounce our protagonist's famous surname the way Gene Wilder does, (as if it ended with the letters "een") which he prefers in an effort to distance himself and his medical research from that of his infamous Transylvanian Grandfather. Unaccustomed to this way of pronouncing his last name, instead, the 'dubbed version of Blücher' accidentally says "Franghenston" in Italian (rendered as Frankenstone in the original version).

In the first of multiple "penis jokes" penned by Wilder and Brooks for this feature film, Inga remarks (00:34:30) that a large creature, as the one Dr. Frankenstein envisioned bringing back to life, would need to also have a very large penis. In Italian, she says "ma allora avrebbe un *enorme* schwanzstück." The original utterance in English is identical in its meaning ("then he would have an *enormous* schwanzstücker"), which the exception of one small detail. The word "schwanzstück" uttered in the dubbed version is an actual German word (lit. "tail piece"), whereas the term "schwanzstücker" used in the Anglophone rendition of the film is not a proper word in German or Yiddish. The intended meaning is clear in either case, yet the usage of a real German word actually reinforces the verisimilitude of the often humorous phonetic and grammatical mistakes made by Inga and Frau Blücher, who always speak with a strong German accent.

About halfway through the film, the doctor has tried without success to reanimate the corpse of a very large individual who had recently been executed by hanging. As the Shelleyan mythos dictates, this attempt involved harnessing the power of lighting to bring this gigantic man (played by

Peter Boyle) back to life. Believing his efforts to be futile, Dr. Frankenstein later hesitates to eat his dinner and discusses his failures with Inga and Igor, who spontaneously mentions what his father used to say in cases like these. In the spirit of some of Brooks' most humorous gags, Igor does not offer any type of anecdotal encouragement or wisdom, but actually alludes to a completely unrelated (and useless) context (00:51:50). Apparently, his father used to shout the following words at him, which suggest that as a young boy Igor spent too much time in the bathroom: "What the hell are you doin' in the bathroom all day and night? Why don't you get out of there and give someone else a chance?". Aside from being completely unexpected, these complaints also raise the possibility that Igor used to lock himself in the bathroom in order to masturbate. The sexual, puerile undertones of this scene are absent in the Italian rendition, though the exchange in question does manage to artfully imply the use of a mildly vulgar word through the use of a broken rhyme scheme. In fact, when Igor quotes his father, he says: "quando la sorte ti è contraria e mancato ti è il successo, smetti di far castelli in aria, e và a piangere sul...." -- a maxim of sorts that is missing the last word "cesso," (meaning "crapper" or "john" as a slang term for toilet) to create a rhyme with the word "successo" (i.e.: "success"). Literally translated, Igor's father's maxim reads "when fate is against you and you have not had success, stop daydreaming and go cry on the... (...crapper)."

When, only a few minutes later, our three characters discover that 'the creature' has indeed been brought back to life, Gene Wilder keeps attempting to instruct them to sedate him, as his own creation is choking him in a moment of panic and disorientation. His repeated attempts to communicate with Igor and Inga with urgency are continuously interrupted by the humongous man's strong grip around his neck, an emergency situation that gives birth to one the most absurd and memorable flights of comedy of the entire film (00:55:20). Twice Dr. Frankenstein yells "Quick! Give him the..." but his breath is cut off right before he can pronounce the word "sedative," so he ends up playing a preposterous game of charades in order to get his point across while also being potentially strangled to death. True in his adherence to the rules of this popular game (given that the doctor is physically incapable of speaking), it is side-splitting to watch him try to suggest the right word one syllable at a time, using hectic hand gestures to avail himself of the "sounds like" option, often employed in the game of charades to "explain" a difficult word by tackling it in small chunks, based on how they sound and other terms they rhyme with. Igor stupidly believes his employer is asking for a "said-a-give," which is enough information for Inga to realize that an injection of a "sedative" is the solution being desperately requested by the protagonist. A parallel operation was carried out in order to offer this linguistic slip-up to viewers in the *Bel Paese*. The principal difference is that Igor's blunder in this case involves the use of the wrong vowel sound ("se-da-TA-vo" instead of "se-da-TI-vo"), but nothing is taken away from the slapstick humor in play, its intensity, or its impact on filmgoers.

In a moment marked by poor judgement and his ambitious desire to have his scientific achievements recognized locally and internationally, Dr. Frankenstein decides to "put on a show" in a Transylvanian theater, placing his reputation at great risk in light of the monster's instability, his rages, and his strong (if not understandable) fear of fire. Although this famous sequence begins much like one of Frankenstein's Medical School lectures as exemplified in the opening portion of the film, once the creature has shown off its basic motor skills the plot makes a deliberate turn towards the ridiculous and completely unexpected with a duet in which the doctor and his creation sing and dance as they perform "Puttin' on the Ritz" (written by Irving Berlin and recorded both by Harry Richman and Fred Astaire in the late 1920s). The song in question marks a radical shift in tone, and its laughable performance may very well be the most preposterous turn of events in the entire plot. Nevertheless, for Italophone viewers who were unfamiliar with Hollywood musicals, translating this song word-for-word would have provided a seemingly useless apparatus in light of their cultural disadvantage (so to speak). Peter Boyle's hilarious falsetto delivers the only two words sung by the creature, or rather: "super duper," which are made to rhyme with Wilder's singing reference to "Gary Cooper." Before the song begins, Dr. Frankenstein promises his audience a "cultured man about town," an utterance that gave birth to the usage (1:20:40) "Dandy in città" in Italian (a dandy about town). Nevertheless, once the singing begins, its lyrics are left untranslated, and this is a choice by the dubbing team that is far from unmotivated.

Inga's most noteworthy mistake in her spoken Italian comes immediately after Dr. Frankenstein's creature shows his true colors by aggressively yelling and gesturing at people in the theater after his failed attempt at singing and dancing. Funnily enough, this instance also allows for her character to accidentally proposition her employer for sex (with yet another "penis joke"), except that in this case her reference to intercourse is entirely unintentional, which certainly adds to the comic tone of the scene in question. In attempting to comfort Wilder's character after his embarrassing and highly public professional failure, Inga kindly mentions that, if she could, she would take "all of his pains" away. In broken Italian, she states (1:23:35) "prenderei tutto tuo pene" which would translate literally as "I would take all your penis."

Since the singular, masculine noun for penis ("pene") is spelled exactly like the plural feminine word for "pains" in Italian, this particular linguistic mistake is dubbed perfectly, reproducing the exact type of comedic and risqué misunderstanding offered in the original English. In fact, Terri Garr's unintended gaffe in English refers to her desire to give Gene Wilder's character "a little peace," which of course is a tongue-in-cheek allusion to the vulgar, sexual, homonymic expression "a little piece," used to refer to female genitalia.

The plot of *Young Frankenstein* is certainly another important factor in the film's translatability: this is a (mostly) straightforward reworking of the story of Dr. Frankenstein and his monster, under the guise of both parody and homage to the classic monster films of the 1930s. As such, the racial problems tackled in *Blazing Saddles* are simply not present or relevant in this film, nor are the cultural problems referenced above. One final aspect that helped lead to the success of this film in Italy involves the individual performances of both the actors and their respective Italian voice actors. The comedy of this film is such that the performances are both more nuanced and more theatrical than in most other comedic pictures directed by Brooks, including *Blazing Saddles*, which was far from successful in Italy.

REFERENCES

http://www.accademiadellacrusca.it/it/lingua-italiana/consulenza-linguistica/domande-risposte/nero-negro-colore. Last visited on July 5, 2018.

Blazing Saddles. Dir. Mel Brooks. Warner Bros. 1974.

Giusti, Marco. *Mel Brooks*. Milano: Il Castoro, 1980.

Santucci, Francesco. "Stornelli Umbri (Dialetto Assisano)," *Lares*, 32. 3/4. 1966. 173-176.

Weide, Robert. "Quiet on the Set! Mel Brooks: the DGA Interview." *DGA Quarterly.* 2012. Los Angeles, CA: Directors Guild
of America, Inc. 30-37.

Young Frankenstein. Dir. Mel Brooks. 20th Century Fox. 1974.

Translating With Subtitles
Lies, Dissimulation, and Censorship in the Works of Moretti, Tornatore, and Pasolini

Daniele Fioretti

Translating is a critical task that involves interactions not only between different languages but, more importantly, between different cultures. Aristotle was maybe the first to emphasize the importance of the act of translation, offering an interpretation that influenced Western thought for centuries. According to the Greek philosopher, words are "affections of the soul" (Aristotle 1984: 25); and since these affections are the same for everyone, it must always be possible to find a way to translate them in different languages. Therefore, starting with Aristotle, Western culture was characterized by an idea of translation based on the transition of meaning from one language to another, and on the confidence in the possibility of perfect translatability. Hence the etymology of the term translation: *translationem* in Latin (nominative *translatio*) means "a carrying across, removal, transporting; transfer of meaning."[1] Of course, even during Aristotle's life translators were aware that the process of translation is complicated by the fact that different languages often do not have a perfect point-to-point correspondence; but the discovery of new lands and the contact with cultures that developed autonomously presented Europeans with new, unforeseen challenges. If these cultures are based on different concepts, unknown in the Old World, how was one to proceed? The idea of perfect translatability was hence called into question, and the entire Aristotelian

---

[1] https://www.etymonline.com/word/translation.

concept of translation had to be reevaluated. Translating became an act marred with potentially unintended consequences and implications, regardless of the specific source and target language(s), as noticed during Romanticism by Friedrich Schleiermacher. Schleiermacher favored an idea of translation that did not try to hide the "foreignness" of the original text; on the contrary, he believed that welcoming foreign elements and structures would be beneficial for the target language (in his case German) because it would lead to an expansion and transformation thereof (1992: 53-54).

Schleiermacher's view was modern and groundbreaking, but it presented a significant drawback: its author did not provide practical criteria or examples of such translations. Furthermore, in spite of its innovative and thought-provoking qualities, Schleiermacher's intuition proved to be very impractical. Usually translators do exactly the opposite; or rather, they actively avoid emphasizing the foreignness of a translation. When they translate from one language to another, they tend to harmonize foreign expressions and concepts, in order to make them understandable to the target audience. This kind of "taming" of a foreign text can have unpredictable repercussions; it may even backfire and impact the source culture; for example, as Loredana Polezzi stated, translation-generated images of Italy eventually made their way back to Italy, influencing Italians' process of self-representation (2009: 263).

Is translation, as many say, an act of betrayal? The well-known Italian expression *traduttore-traditore* (i.e.: *translator-traitor*) seems to validate this idea; but the problem is: who is the translator betraying or, more specifically, to whom should s/he pledge allegiance? To the source culture or to the target culture? The point in question is that a translator is a mediator between cultures, but this mediation is not without risks, especially when source and target cultures differ significantly. The safest way to translate, of course, is to be as literal as possible. Following the taxonomy proposed by the Canadian linguists Jean-Paul Vinay and Jean D'Albernet in 1958, translations can be direct (literal) or oblique. The procedures of direct translation described by the two scholars — borrowing, calque, and literal translation — do not pose relevant problems. The second category instead is much more challenging. Oblique translations, for Vinay and D'Albernet, include transposition (replacing one word class with another without changing the meaning of the message), modulation (a variation obtained with a change in point of view), equivalence (when the same notion can be rendered with completely different stylistic and structural methods), and adaptation (where the concept exposed in the source language text is unknown in the target language, and is replaced by another that the translator considers "equivalent"). Adaptation is defined by our Canadian scholars a "situational equivalence" (Vinay and D'Albernet 2004: 134-135). The example they make is rather extreme. In British culture, it is culturally acceptable for a man to kiss his daughter on the lips, while in French culture this is unacceptable. Therefore, translating a text from English to French, the translator should write that the father holds his daughter tenderly in his arms, instead of kissing her, so to avoid cultural misinterpretations (Vinay and D'Albernet 2004: 134).

This kind of translation is rather extreme. Is adaptation a betrayal, then, or a lie? In his essay on lies, Jacques Derrida examined the Greek expression *pseudos* which "can mean lie, as well as falsehood, cunning or mistake, and deception or fraud as well as poetic invention" (Derrida 1997: 130). Even if the meaning of the word suggests the possibility of a connection between intentional acts, mistakes, and fiction, Derrida immediately clarified that an error cannot be classified as a lie, and that the act of lying is something different from mistakes and self-deception. Could one say something that is not true without lying? The answer is yes, provided that the "liar" is speaking in good faith, fully believing s/he has made an honest statement. In order to define someone who says untrue things as a liar, it is necessary to look at their intentions. As Augustine wrote in *De mendacio*, the bearer of false news, if acting in good faith, is not a liar. On the contrary, someone may lie even by saying the truth; that is, saying something true but with the intention of deceiving (Augustine 1952: 54-55). Jean-Jacques Rousseau agrees, but only in part. In his *Reveries of a Solitary Walker*, Rousseau stated that the intention of deceit is necessary in order to lie, but he also claimed that untrue statements, which do not harm the self or others, cannot be classified as lies, but as fiction (Rousseau 1783: 195). In other words, Rousseau started shifting the focus from the intentionality of the liar to the effects that the false statement produces. If a lie is harmless, as he stated, it cannot be qualified as a lie.

Another relevant problem arises from this discourse however: how can one assess or quantify the harm produced by a lie? The assessment of the harm caused by a lie — or by an unfaithful translation — is based on the point of view of the interpreter; and if we move the discussion to the field of translation, can we describe an unfaithful translation as a lie or merely as fiction? We cannot deny that translating is a voluntary, deliberate act, but can it represent a form of dishonesty? It is a fact that literal translations are not always sufficient to transfer the meaning of a text, literary or cinematic, from one language to another. There are some idiomatic constructions and cultural frameworks that are remarkably difficult to translate into another linguistic system.

There are of course other ways to solve this problem without resorting to such an extreme form of adaptation. For example, in a written text the translator or the editor can include footnotes or endnotes to clarify a problematic passage. In the case described by Vinay and D'Albernet, a simple footnote detailing how the circumstance of a father kissing a daughter on the lips is perfectly acceptable in British culture should be sufficient. It mainly depends on the type of text and its intended audience. If the text to be translated is a popular fiction novel it is unlikely that the readers would be interested in lengthy cultural explanations. However, if the translator works on a treatise or an essay intended for a scholarly audience, s/he would probably prefer to make only minimal interventions on the text, possibly adding para-textual information (such as footnotes) to give the reader all the data needed to understand the text correctly.

The situation is considerably different when the work being translated is a motion picture as opposed to a literary text. Slavoj Žižek reported some humorous examples that show the risks of an extreme cultural adaptation; for example, in the Japanese version of *Gone with the Wind*, Rhett Butler (played by Clark Gable) does not say "Frankly, my dear, I don't give a damn!" since, to respect Japanese etiquette, the line was changed to "I fear, my darling, that there is a slight misunderstanding between the two of us." Even more clearly, the famous final line of *Casablanca*, "This is the beginning of a beautiful friendship," was translated in Chinese with: "The two of us will now constitute a new cell of anti-fascist struggle" (Žižek 2009: 8). As we can see, the translation tends to emphasize the political content instead of more personal themes like friendship. Furthermore, it is clear that in these cases there is an exaggerated emphasis of the rules governing the use of the target culture, which in turn has the effect of taming the foreignness of the translated text. This level of intervention is very problematic: adaptation as cultural equivalence can be seen as a practice straddling the border between translation and interpretation, and maybe even a form of lying: an innocent lie maybe, one that, according to Rousseau, should not be considered a lie at all.

Cinematic translations are carried out in two ways: with dubbing or subtitles. Germany, Italy, France, and Spain, for example, are mainly dubbing-nations, while subtitling is the mostly typical form of translation in the United States, the UK, the Benelux Union, Scandinavian countries, Greece and Portugal (Chiaro 2009: 147). Subtitles are, by necessity, strictly dependent on the timing of the images; the written text should be shorter than the corresponding portion of the language track because viewers must have the time to read the subtitles without being too distracted from the plot of the movie and, possibly, without being aware that they are reading. Often, especially when a film is dominated by dialogue, the original exchanges are heavily reduced (Antonini 2005: 213). This process includes the elimination of elements like false starts, hesitations, slang and dialect, as well as the simplification of the original syntax, so as to make reading simpler and quicker. Typically, subtitles are placed on the bottom of the frame in one or two lines, and they should be no more than 40 characters, spaces included (Chiaro 2009: 149). The average exposure time is around 3-6 seconds (Linde and Kay 1999: 7), a duration that is considered comfortable even for slower readers who are not familiar with the source language.

One of the most interesting features of this form of translation is that subtitling is a translation operating across different forms of media, given that oral speech is rendered in a written form. This characteristic implies a number of additional challenges; in fact, it is difficult, if not impossible, to translate non-verbal communication with subtitles, because of the aforementioned constraints. However, the art of subtitling offers a significant advantage for the spectator, as it neither conceals nor distorts the original version. The original dialogues can be still heard, and this is a factor that may represent an additional challenge for the translator. In fact, unlike other forms of translation, subtitling potentially allows for the cross-examination of the work of the translator, provided that the spectators are proficient in both languages.

A critical point in subtitling is the translation of humor and taboo language, that is, words or expressions related to sex or considered inappropriate for a variety of other reasons. Taboo words may be censored in a translation, but they are still audible and available for an audience that is able to recognize them. However, offensive or inappropriate terms are — if not totally erased — often reduced in subtitling more than in dubbing (Chiaro 2009: 151). Two famous Italian movies produced between the end of the 1980s and the beginning of the 1990s are very telling under this respect: Nanni Moretti's *Caro Diario* (1993) and Giuseppe Tornatore's *Nuovo Cinema Paradiso* (1988). In both feature films, in fact, we find examples of the use of a very controversial term, the Italian word *negro*, which is now perceived as offensive in Italian as the 'N-word' is in English, but which, at the time of their release, was still used in modern Italian to refer to black people without any racist or negative implications, as confirmed by a study of the Accademia della Crusca.[2]

At the beginning of *Caro Diario* Moretti is riding his Vespa in the empty streets of Rome, while the director's voice-over says:

---

[2]http://www.accademiadellacrusca.it/it/lingua-italiana/consulenza-linguistica/domande-risposte/nero-negro-colore.

> D'estate a Roma i cinema sono tutti chiusi. Oppure ci sono film
> come *Sesso, amore e pastorizia, Desideri bestiali, Biancaneve e i sette
> negri*, oppure qualche film dell'orrore come *Henry*, oppure qual-
> che film italiano.

> [In the summer in Rome the cinemas are all closed. Or there are
> movies like *Sex, Love and Ship-farming, Beastly Desires, Snow White
> and the Seven Blacks*, or some horror film like *Henry*, or some Ital-
> ian film].

Nanni Moretti, of course, was not trying to be offensive to
black people; he wanted to show how disappointed he was at
the lack of good movies one could see in Rome during the
summer. The first three titles probably refer to real porn movies, screened at that time in dedicated *cinema a luci rosse*, X-
rated movie theaters. *Henry: Portrait of a Serial Killer* (John
McNaughton, 1986), gives Moretti the chance for a tirade
against some film reviewers whose work is published in
newspapers. The reference to porn movies is meant to emphasize the negative judgement Moretti attributes to the distribution of films in Italy at that time, but the translation considerably softens the original, particularly in the case of the
third movie, translated as *Snow White and the Seven Blacks*. On
the one hand, the choice of using "blacks" instead of the 'N-
word' is reasonable, because it helps to avoid misunderstandings with an English-speaking audience; on the other hand,
this choice makes Moretti's speech sound less scandalous,
therefore less effective and less poignant in its condemnation.
Instead of a caustic remark against Italian movie distributors,
the speech sounds uninfluential, if not pointless.

The use of taboo language is much more extensive in
Giuseppe Tornatore's *Nuovo Cinema Paradiso* (1988), perhaps
in an effort to render the colloquial tone of the speech patterns
of the inhabitants of the small town of Giancaldo. There are

frequent references to sex in the dialogues of this movie, and the subtitles usually translate them with punctual accuracy: for example, the military joke that Totò tells Alfredo about the colonel's daughter's rear end ("Signorina, se avete il cuore duro come ciò che ho toccato adesso sono un uomo finito!", translated as "If your heart is as hard as what I just felt, I'm a dead man!"), or the comment made by Totò's friends about Elena's upper-class family ("Quella è gente che la minchia se la toccano con la camicia per non sporcarsi le mani," translated with "He jerks off with his shirt, not to get his hands dirty"). When, in other cases, the text is changed, the intention seems to avoid the use of gratuitous profanity, or to replace untranslatable plays on words and idiomatic expressions. One very strange case is when Ciccio Spaccafico, also known in the movie as "Spaccafico the Neapolitan," was arguing with a film distributor (Titanus) about a movie that was very popular at the end of the 1940s, *Catene* by Raffaele Matarazzo, (1949). Apparently, the distributor wanted the copy of the movie back after only two days, which was not enough time to fulfill the requests of the audience of Giancaldo. This is why Spaccafico decided to show the movie in two theaters, alternating part one and part two, with the help of Boccia, a friend of Totò, who rushes back and forth from one movie theater to another riding his bike. In the scene Spaccafico is speaking on the phone, so we cannot hear what the interlocutor is saying, but the substance is clear:

> Solo due giorni? Ma a chi volete sfottere? E che me ne frega se le copie sono impegnate? *Catene* solo due giorni? Ma qua la gente mi mangerà gli occhi! Sì, lo so, lo so, ma anche se comincio lo spettacolo alle otto di mattina non ce la faccio! Il paese è grande e voi della Titanus lo sapete. E se mi fate incazzare io scrivo a Lombardo a Roma. Il Risorgimento vi faccio vedere! Io mi chia-

mo Spaccafico, ma se mi girano i coglioni vi spacco pure le corna!

[Only one print? You know I need one for the Paradiso, one for
the next town. You promised. I put up posters, made commit-
ments! If you screw me, watch out! One print for two theaters.
You'll pay for this! I'm from Naples, and you will see it and die!]

The subtitled text, as we said before, has been shortened
and simplified in comparison to the Italian version for clarity
and brevity, but it conveys effectively the sense of urgency
and the comic rage of Spaccafico. While making these changes, the translator avoided many of the profanities used in the
original speech and then, unable to render in English the expression "io vi spacco le corna" (meaning "I will break your
skull," but with an implicit reference to cuckoldry, since
"avere le corna," to wear horns, in colloquial Italian means to
be a cuckold), the translator preferred to convey the sense of
an old saying, "vedi Napoli e poi muori!" ("see Naples and
then die!"). The translation is rather goofy and lacks in effica-
cy, but it does not alter the sense of the scene. There are some
changes in the film related to ethnically sensitive expressions
that were commonly used in Italy in the 1950s and 1960s but
could have been perceived as offensive by an English-
speaking audience. In these cases the translator decided to
remove these references completely. For example, in a scene
the ticket collector and usher of the movie theater (played by
Leo Gullotta) complains that the spectators are smoking too
much saying "[C]ome i turchi fumano, come i turchi!" The
literal translation refers to an old Italian expression, "to
smoke like a Turk," based on the stereotype that — apparently — Turks are heavy smokers. The English translation
("They smoke like chimneys!") eliminates the potentially offensive ethnic reference, which would make no sense for an

English-speaking spectator anyway. But, as previously stated, in *Cinema Paradiso*, like in *Dear Diary*, there is a problematic reference to black people, when young Totò is at home playing with film cutouts stolen from Alfredo's film booth:

Ehi tu, lurido bastardo, cala giù le mani dall'oro. Sporco negro, stai alla larga da me, sennò ti rompo la faccia.

[Hey, you! Dirty swine, hands off that gold! Blackhearted pig, stay away from me or I'll smash your face in].

In this case the reference to black people is unequivocally offensive and unmotivated: the audience cannot see the images on the cutouts, so the subtitler was wise to change the 'N-word' to "blackhearted pig," which is not an ethnic or racial insult. Maybe we can consider these changes as adaptations, in the sense proffered by Vinay and D'Albernet, or perhaps as "innocent lies" (in the words of Rousseau), or as examples of *dissimulazione onesta* (honest dissimulation), a reference to the treatise *Della dissimulazione onesta* written by Torquato Accetto in 1641. Accetto, who lived in the Kingdom of Naples in the 17th century under Spanish dominion, emphasized in his work the need for the courtier to be prudent in troubled times in order to avoid censorship and repression. It is interesting to note that Accetto did not advocate lying (simulating), but instead he suggested one keep silent and refrain from expressing the truth in its entirety, "non essendo altro il dissimulare che un velo composto di tenebre oneste e di rispetti violenti: da che non si forma il falso, ma si dà qualche riposo al vero, per dimostrarlo a tempo" (not being the dissimulation anything but a veil composed of honest darkness and violent respects: from which one does not create falsity, but gives some rest to the truth, so as to reveal it at the right time) (Accetto 2016: 23, my translation). If we accept this interpretation, these mistranslations may very well represent a dissimulation of elements that are not necessary to comprehend a film as a whole, but that can soften the impact of sensitive cultural contrasts.

The cases of cultural adaptation discussed thus far can be easily classified as innocent lies or dissimulations. However, there are other examples of translation through subtitling that appear much more disingenuous and may reveal a hidden political agenda, like the 1963 subtitled version of the short film *La ricotta* by Pier Paolo Pasolini. In order to better understand this example, one must first consider Pasolini as a cultural figure and the way his literary and cinematic works were received in the 1960s and 1970s. Pasolini is now considered one of the most important and influential Italian intellectuals of the 20th century, but public opinion in the 1960s painted a very different image of this poet, writer, and filmmaker. Pasolini's novels and movies were considered extremely scandalous, like the public persona of the author himself. One of the reasons why Pasolini was perceived as such a controversial figure is that he never tried to hide his homosexuality, at a time when homosexuals were considered by the majority of society as sick or perverted individuals. Furthermore, in his books and movies Pasolini often focused on marginal realities, such as the lives of sub-proletarians in the slums of Rome, including petty criminals and prostitutes. These people with no future, who were mostly ignored by the mainstream culture, were represented in a graphic, violent way. Instead of catching the substance of Pasolini's underlying social condemnation of the hypocrisy in mainstream Italian society, many people (including a significant number of critics and intellectuals) saw Pasolini as a filthy individual, a pervert who was morbidly attracted to crime and abjection.

Even from an ideological point of view Pasolini did not fit in a specific category: he was a self-professed communist, but a "heretical" one, often in contrast with the official cultural line of the Italian Communist Party (PCI) and therefore harshly criticized both by right-wing newspapers and left-wing intellectuals. Furthermore, even if he declared himself an atheist, Pasolini made frequent references to religion and religious figures in his poems, novels, and movies, which garnered him highly critical remarks both from religious conservatives who thought that the atheist Pasolini was mocking religion, and by many left-wing activists who saw these references as a resurgence of religious spiritualism. Speaking of religion, Pasolini was particularly attracted by extreme, radical figures like Jesus and Saint Francis of Assisi, as he saw a strong connection between their rejection of personal property and material possessions and his own communist ideals. Finally, the idea of sex as an anti-capitalistic, liberating force, which is explicit in movies like *Teorema* (1968), *The Decameron* (1971), *The Canterbury Tales* (1972), and *Arabian Nights* (1974), was the cause of numerous controversies and legal charges of obscenity. Ever since the release of his first movie (*Accattone*, 1961) Pasolini was the target of what Guido Bonsaver called "censorship by trial" (Bonsaver 2014: 70). Even worse, if possible, was the reception of *La ricotta*, which was distributed as an episode of the movie *RoGoPaG* (1963), along with three other short movies made by Roberto Rossellini, Jean-Luc Godard and Ugo Gregoretti. The movie was immediately confiscated by the authorities, and Pasolini was formally accused of offending Italy's national religion.

Why did the prosecuting attorney Giuseppe Di Gennaro level this charge (for the first time in the history of the Italian republic) against Pasolini? *La ricotta* is a meta-cinematic movie, that is, a movie on the making of a movie (on the Passion

of Christ), where Stracci (a starving extra who plays the part
of the good thief) dies on the cross, surrounded by the indifference of the film crew. Pasolini's main goal was to show
that the tragedy of Christ (under a layman's point of view),
symbolized by the immolation of an innocent victim, happens
every day thousands of times in front of our very eyes and we
are unable to see it. This important facet was lost on the pros-
ecutor, who accused Pasolini of blasphemy and contempt towards the Catholic faith. The author's intention was quite the
opposite though, as noted by Maurizio Viano: "Pasolini's film
may seem the impious vision of a blasphemous eye when, in
reality, it aspires to denounce commercial speculation just as
Christ denounced the moneylenders in the temple [...]
Whereas the expensive production of Christ's Passion fails to
reproduce the feeling of its alleged object, the ridiculed Stracci
is the true inheritor of the cross" (Viano 1993: 103). Due to
these charges Pasolini was initially sentenced to four months
in jail and later acquitted.

Because of the fame and the artistic quality of the directors
involved in the project, and perhaps also as a result of the up-
roar caused by the confiscation of the movie, *RoGoPaG* was
presented at the first New York Film Festival on September of
1963 and the following month at the London Film Festival,
but it was never distributed in movie theaters in the US nor in
the UK.[3] The first translation with English subtitles of the
movie, therefore, must have been done purposefully for these
American and British screenings. We know that Pasolini did
not approve of subtitles at all. In an interview given in 1970
Pasolini defended his choice to dub Maria Callas in the movie
Medea, and on that occasion he also talked about subtitles in

---

[3] I am indebted to Roberto Chiesi, Director of the Centro Studi - Archivio Pier
Paolo Pasolini, Cineteca di Bologna, for sharing the aforementioned information
regarding the subtitling and screening of *RoGoPaG.*

general. According to Pasolini subtitles ruin the aesthetic quality of a film, covering a substantial portion of the shot:

> A good dubbing is less annoying for me than subtitles, because the subtitles disfigure the image. Now, when I create an image I choose a shot, then I torment the cinematographer for half an hour, I beg him: 'Keep the image in that point, straighten it up, in this way'. Then I see a subtitle that covers everything. It's a horrible, unbearable thing, I can't stand subtitles ... The subtitle disfigures the image, there's nothing to do, it changes the sense of the image (Pasolini 2001: 2789, my translation).

Pasolini probably never saw *La ricotta* with English subtitles; otherwise he would have been even more frustrated than usual. In fact, if compared to the subtitles made for the Criterion DVD edition of *Mamma Roma* in 2004, which includes *La ricotta* in its special features, there are remarkable differences in play which are puzzling and difficult to justify. It is true, as we said, that the task of the subtitler is an arduous one. Subtitles must respect the duration of the speech in the movie. They can't be fully explanatory, they must transmit to the audience the meaning of the dialogue very rapidly, without distracting the moviegoer from the content of the film. No footnotes are allowed, nor prefatory notes of any kind. However, there are cases in which the shifts in meaning cannot be exclusively attributed to these constraints. The subtitles made in 1963 for *La ricotta* are a prime example of the fact that often, in a translation, the foreign text is rewritten according to the terms and values of the target culture (Venuti 2004: 112). Subtitling, wrote Abé Mark Nornes, "because of the violent reduction of the translation demanded by the apparatus, is a method of translation that conspires to hide its work — along with its ideological assumptions — from its own reader-spectators" (Nornes 2004: 449). The 1963 translation of *La ri-*

cotta is emblematic of a kind of translation that is so intensely concerned with the response of the audience that it makes questionable adaptations to the original text, especially in the scene of the interview, where a servile journalist asks a handful of routine questions to the director of the movie on the Passion of Christ. At the end of the interview, the director reads a segment from a poem written by Pasolini himself, and finally accuses the journalist of being an "average man": "Ma lei non sa cos'è un uomo medio? È un mostro. Un pericoloso delinquente. Conformista! Colonialista! Razzista! Schiavista! Qualunquista!"

The translation of many of these adjectives in English does not appear to be problematic: *mostro* is "monster" in both translations (1963 and 2004), just like *pericoloso delinquente* is rendered in both translations as "dangerous criminal." *Conformista* does not pose specific problems, and in fact both translations say "conformist." The same can be said for *colonialista,* translated as "colonialist"; *schiavista* in 1963 is translated as "slave dealer," in 2004 as "slave trader" with no noteworthy change in meaning. *Qualunquista* is, however, a more problematic term. In English-Italian dictionaries this term is frequently translated as "politically indifferent person" or "politically cynical." For an Italian audience, however, especially in 1963, the term also referred to the antipolitical movement "Fronte dell'Uomo Qualunque" (FUQ), founded in 1944 by the journalist Guglielmo Giannini. Even if this movement was not openly fascist (ex-fascists veterans of the "Repubblica di Salò" founded the "Movimento Sociale Italiano," also known as MSI), the militants of the Fronte dell'Uomo Qualunque were right-wing conservatives who manifested disdain for the new political system and fought, on two fronts, against communism as well as industrial capitalism. When Pasolini used this term he clearly wanted to allude to both meanings of the word *qualunquista*. However, if the 2004 subtitles translate this word as "a mediocrity," which is an acceptable translation, the 1963 subtitles, surprisingly, translate *qualunquista* with "socialist," which is a very questionable solution to say the least. If we take *qualunquista* only to mean "politically indifferent person," then the use of the term "socialist" is undoubtedly erroneous. If we consider this usage only in political terms, then the actual meaning is exactly the opposite of the translation offered in 1963. Socialists and communists were among the worst enemies of FUQ. A possible (but unlikely) explanation is that the translator was totally ignorant of the term's true meaning and unaware of its political implications, so s/he decided to use a word that, during the Cold War and the anti-communist witch-hunt that accompanied it, represented the ultimate evil for many Americans: socialism. If this is the case, said translation could be considered a bad example of "adaptation," in the sense suggested by Vinay and D'Albernet: "it is used in those cases where the type of situation being referred to by the SL [Source Language] message is unknown in the TL [Target Language] culture" (2004: 134-135). Nevertheless, this hypothesis of the extreme use of a situational equivalence is not very persuasive, because other terms in the same scene have been translated strangely. For example, the word *razzista*, translated rather obviously with "racist" in the subtitles made in 2004, in 1963 subtitles had been translated with "nationalist," another controversial and apparently unmotivated choice. Are we to believe that all nationalists are racist and vice-versa? The translator clearly avoided the most logical, literal option (i.e.: "racist"). We can formulate another hypothesis, though — or an educated guess: maybe the topic was considered too divisive in the American political climate of 1963, the same year when Martin Luther King

Jr. organized the Civil Rights Movement's "March on Washington for Jobs and Freedom." After all, in the same days when *RoGoPaG* was screened in New York a Baptist church in Selma, Alabama was bombed, killing four black children. In any case, the concurrence of these two bizarre mistranslations is suspicious, yet there are other inaccuracies that seem to suggest a not-so-hidden political agenda. When the character of the journalist, in the course of the interview, asks the director his opinion on death, the latter responds: "Come marxista, è un fatto che non prendo in considerazione." Not surprisingly, the 2004 subtitles correctly render the sentence with: "As a Marxist, I never give it any thought." However, the 1963 version of the subtitles differed significantly: "It is a fact to which I never gave a thought." The term "Marxist" had simply been excised. It is rather difficult, in light of this evidence, not to view these mistranslations as the result of an ideological strategy, one that was intent on censoring specific political connotations that would have been poorly received and easily misunderstood by an Anglophone audience in the United States. This scene in *La ricotta,* as it was screened in 1963, had been purged of any term that made reference to Pasolini's leftist political views, up to the point that a self-proclaimed Marxist was made to say that the average man is a socialist. In this case, though, the translator did not detect Pasolini's irony: through the (fictional) director's words, the author was not adamantly expressing his own political views; but rather, he was criticizing the fundamental views held by Marxists.

The notion of death, unlike his political viewpoints, is present in almost every movie made by Pasolini. Not only Stracci, but also the protagonist of *Accattone* dies at the end of the movie. Ettore, for example, the son of the main character in *Mamma Roma* (1962), dies in bed in prison, and the image of his dead body is clearly intended as an iconographic allusion to Andrea Mantegna's famous painting *Lamento sul Cristo morto* (produced around the year 1478). Pasolini, in fact, in his 1967 essay *Osservazioni sul piano-sequenza*, wrote that death makes a sudden *montage* of our entire lives and makes them understandable and linguistically describable (Pasolini 1999: 1560).

It is hence clear that death is a central theme for Pasolini; so his intention was not to mock Catholicism, but to criticize orthodox Marxists, who do not take into account anything beyond materialism. As Viano wrote: "*La ricotta* thus informs us of the director's political beliefs but also puts Pasolini's finger on one of Marxism's weak points, its refusal to acknowledge death as a worthwhile subject for theoretical reflection" (1993: 105). Pasolini, far from expressing a materialistic point of view, suggested that a certain typology of Marxism should be more "spiritual" and open to left-wing Catholics, the ones who — at that time in Italy — were called *cattocomunisti* (Catholic-communists).

There is one last example worth noting of the problematic strategy employed in the subtitles used in 1963: during the interview the director asks the journalist if he suffers from heart disease. When the latter answers in the negative, the director replies:

Peccato, perché se mi crepava qui davanti sarebbe stato un buon elemento per il lancio del film. Tanto lei non esiste. Il capitale non considera esistente la manodopera se non quando serve alla produzione. E il produttore del mio film è anche il padrone del suo giornale.

[Too bad, because if you had dropped dead right here, it would have been good publicity for the film's release. You don't exist anyway. Capital acknowledges the existence of labor only inso-

far as it serves production. And the producer of my film is the
owner of your paper as well]. (*La ricotta,* subtitles 2004)

Here Pasolini is openly political: the director's speech
seems taken directly from Marx's text *The Capital*; but in the
1963 version the most suggestive political term, "capital," was
translated with the far more neutral noun "producer." The
result is the following: "the producer regards you as existing
only if you serve the production, because the producer of my
film is the owner of your paper!" (*La ricotta,* subtitles 1963).
Again, any explicit political reference has been removed from
the translation in this case.

Should the 1963 subtitles of *La ricotta* be considered a case
of adaptation, in the sense put forth by Vinay and D'Albernet,
or perhaps an extreme case of "dynamic equivalence," as per
Eugene Nida's terminology (2003: 156)? These types of pragmatic equivalences or adaptations often conceal a hidden political agenda. The case of *La ricotta* is rather extreme in this
sense: more than dissimulation or innocent lies, it appears
that the translator made an intentional effort to deceive the
audience, hiding Pasolini's political views and their implications. In general, if it is true that every translation tends to reduce the "otherness" of a foreign work of art, in order to
make it available, accessible, and acceptable to a domestic audience in a different cultural framework, it follows that excessive domestications that tend to distort or misrepresent the
message of the written or cinematic text should be avoided at
all costs. In this sense one should make a point to bear in
mind Antoine Berman's concept of an "ethic of translation"
(2004: 285). According to Berman, translators have a moral
responsibility in their work. Biased translations — like the
one we have just examined — do not simply domesticate the
text, they have a mystifying effect because of their systemic

negation of the foreignness of the original text, even from a political point of view. Mystification can and should be seen as a form of deception. It is necessary for the translator to become aware of his/her moral responsibility and avoid any ethnocentric or nationalistic impulses or inclinations: any translated work should maintain its foreignness to avoid the risk of contributing to a process of cultural annexation (Berman 2004: 286).

Unfortunately, there are no translations that do not run, at least potentially, the risk of becoming too ethnocentric. As Lawrence Venuti wrote, every translation is always ideological, because it implies the risk of a potential imperialistic strategy. If, according to Venuti, the ethnocentric violence of translation is inevitable, because "in the translating process, foreign languages, texts, and cultures will always undergo some degree and form of reduction, exclusion, inscription" (Venuti 1995: 310), there is a possible escape from this mechanism, which is to leave the foreign text's "otherness" intact. Only in this way can translation become the subverter of the empire, and not its agent (Venuti 2004: 220).

REFERENCES

Accattone. Dir. Pier Paolo Pasolini. Arco Film. 1961.

Accetto, Torquato. *Della dissimulazione onesta* (1641). Milano: Rizzoli, 2016.

Antonini, Rachele. "The Perception of Subtitled Humor in Italy." *Humor*, 18, 2, 2005. 209-225.

Arabian Nights. Dir. Pier Paolo Pasolini. Produzione Europee Associate. 1974.

Aristotle. *The Complete Works of Aristotle*, vol. I. Princeton: Princeton University Press, 1984.

Augustine. "Lying." *The Fathers of the Church, Volume 16*. Ed. Roy J. Deferrari. Washington: The Catholic University of America Press, 1952. 45-110.

Berman, Antoine. "Translations and Other Trials of the Foreign." *The Translation Study Reader*. Ed. Lawrence Venuti. New York-London: Routledge, 2004. 284-297.

Bonsaver, Guido. "Censorship from the Fascist Period to the Present." *The Italian Cinema Book*. Ed. Peter Bondanella. London: Palgrave Macmillan, 2014. 66-74.

The Canterbury Tales. Dir. Pier Paolo Pasolini. Produzioni Europee Associate. 1972.

Caro Diario. Dir. Nanni Moretti. Sacher Film. 1993.

Casablanca. Dir. Michael Curtiz. Warner Bros. 1942.

Catene. Dir. Raffaele Matarazzo. Labor Film. 1949.

Chiaro, Delia. "Issues in Audiovisual Translation." *The Routledge Companion to Translation Studies*. Ed. Jeremy Munday. Oxon: Routledge, 2009. 141-165.

The Decameron. Dir. Pier Paolo Pasolini. Produzioni Europee Associate. 1971.

Derrida, Jacques. "History of the Lie: Prolegomena." *Graduate Faculty Philosophy Journal*, 19-20, 1-2, 1997. 129-61.

Gone with the Wind. Dir. Victor Fleming. Selznick International Pictures. 1930.

Henry: Portrait of a Serial Killer. Dir. John McNaughton. Maljack Productions. 1986.

Linde, Zoe de, and Neil Kay. *The Semiotics of Subtitling*. Manchester: St. Jerome, 1999.

Mamma Roma. Dir. Pier Paolo Pasolini. Arco Film. 1964.

Nida, Eugene A, and Charles R. Taber. *The Theory and Practice of Translation*. Leiden and Boston: Brill, 2003.

Nation, Language and the Ethics of Translation. Eds. Sandra Bermann and Michael Wood. Princeton and Oxford: Princeton University Press, 2005.

Nornes, Abé Mark. "For an Abusive Subtitling." *The Translation Study Reader*. Ed. Lawrence Venuti. New York and London: Routledge, 2004. 447-469.

Nuovo cinema paradiso. Dir. Giuseppe Tornatore. Cristaldifilm. 1988.

Pasolini, Pier Paolo. *Per il cinema*. Milano: Mondadori, 2001.

_____. *Saggi sulla letteratura e sull'arte*. Milano: Mondadori, 1999.

Polezzi, Loredana. "Reflections of Things Past: Building Italy Through the Mirror of Translation." *Routledge Encyclopedia of Translation Studies*. Eds. Mona Baker and Gabriela Saldanha. Abingdon: Routledge, 2009. 262-282.

La Ricotta. Dir. Pier Paolo Pasolini. Cineriz. 1963.

Rousseau, Jean-Jacques. *The Confessions,* with the *Reveries of a Solitary Walker*. London: Bew, 1783.

Schleiermacher, Friedrich. "On the Different Methods of Translating." *Theories of Translation. An Anthology of Essays from Dryden to Deridda*. Ed. Rainer Schulter and John Biguenet. Chicago: University of Chicago Press, 1992. 36-54.

Subini, Tomaso. *Pier Paolo Pasolini: La ricotta*. Torino: Landau, 2009.

Teorema. Dir. Pier Paolo Pasolini. Aetos Produzioni Cinematografiche. 1968.

Tonelli, Anna. *Per indegnità morale. Il caso Pasolini nell'Italia del buoncostume*. Roma-Bari: Laterza, 2015.

Venuti, Lawrence. *The Translator's Invisibility. A History of Translation*. New York-London: Routledge, 1995.

Venuti, Lawrence, Ed. *The Translation Studies Reader*. New York and London: Routledge, 2004.

Viano, Maurizio. *A Certain Realism. Making Use of Pasolini's Film Theory and Practice*. Berkelcy: University of California Press, 1993.

Vinay, Jean-Paul and Jean D'Albernet. "A Methodology for Translation." *The Translation Study Reader*. Ed. Lawrence Venuti. New York and London: Routledge, 2004. 128-137.

Žižek, Slavoy. *In Defense of Lost Causes*. London and New York: Verso, 2009.

CONTRIBUTORS

PHILIP BALMA (Ph.D. Indiana University) is Associate Professor of Italian Literary and Cultural Studies at the University of Connecticut-Storrs, where he serves as the director of the undergraduate program in Italian Studies and the co-chair of Film Studies. His work on modern Italian film and literature has appeared in numerous journals in the US and Europe, including *Italica, Forum Italicum, Italian Quarterly, Translation Review, Incontri: Rivista Europea di Studi Italiani, Saggi di 'Lettere Italiane', Translation Studies Journal* and *Luci e ombre: rivista bimestrale di informazione cinematografica e culturale.* His most recent publications include *Edith Bruck in the Mirror: Fictional Transitions and Cinematic Narratives* (Purdue UP, 2014) and *The Jewish Experience in Contemporary Italy.* Spec. Iss. of *Nemla Italian Studies* 37 (2015).

LUCA BARATTONI (Ph.D. University of North Carolina, Chapel Hill) is Associate Professor of Italian at Clemson University. Among his publications: *Italian Post-Neorealist Cinema* (Edinburgh: Edinburgh UP, 2012); "Revanscismo e nazionalismo dei generi neo-folk e Oi! alla luce delle sottoculture musicali italiane" in Alessandro Carrera, ed., *La memoria delle canzoni: Popular Music e identità italiana* (Novi Ligure: Puntoacapo, 2016); "*Edipo Re* e lo statuto del soggetto" in F. Orsitto & F. Pacchioni, eds., *Pier Paolo Pasolini: Prospettive Americane* (Pesaro: Metauro, 2015).

RICHARD BONANNO (Ph.D. Rutgers University) is Associate Professor of Italian at Assumption College. Among his publications: "What to Learn from a Tale of Building a 'Campus' and Academic Program in Italy," *Beyond* 1 (2018); "Interview with Joe Castiglione, the Voice of the Boston Red Sox," *Italian Americana,* Summer 2018; "Cloistered Bodies and Open Minds in Boccaccio's *Decameron*" in M. Marino & G. Spani, eds., *Donne del Mediterraneo. Saggi Interdisciplinari* (Firenze: Società Editrice Fiorentina, 2017); H. Giusto, ed., *Daesh and the Terrorist Threat: from the Middle East to Europe.* Trans. Richard Bonanno (Brussels: Foundation for European Progressive Studies/Fondazione Italianieuropei, 2015)

ELEONORA BUONOCORE (Ph.D. Yale University; Ph.D. Università degli Studi di Siena) is a member of the Italian Faculty at the University of Calgary. She has previously taught Italian Language and Literature at Yale University, the University of Notre Dame and Colby College. Her publications include: "The Other Model: Siena as a Purgatorial City in Dante" in *Vedere nell'ombra Studi su natura, spiritualità e scienze operative offerti a Michela Pereira* (Firenze: SISMEL Edizioni del Galluzzo (2018), 131-142; "The *Loyca discipuli magistri Raymondi Lulli*: Introducing an Introduction to Lullian Logic at the End of the 14th c." in *Il Lullismo in Italia: itinerario storico critico*. Palermo: Officina di studi medievali; Roma: Antonianum, 2015, 71-91; and "The Ur-text of Late Medieval and Renaissance Lullian Logic. Textual Interrelations Between the Nove introductiones and Two Traditional Pseudo-Lullian Handbooks of Logic: The Logica parva and the Logica brevis et nova." *Studia Lulliana* 53 (2013): 23-66.

FELICE ITALO BENEDUCE (Ph.D. University of Connecticut) is Senior Lecturer of Italian, Columbia University. Prior to joining Columbia University, Beneduce taught Italian literature and cinema and Italian-American literature and cinema at Trinity College, the University of Connecticut, Brown University, Providence College and the University of Rhode Island. Among his publications: S. Lazzarin, F. I. Beneduce et al. *Il fantastico italiano. Bilancio critico e bibliografia commentata (dal 1980 a oggi)* (Milan: Mondadori Education-Le Monnier Università, 2016); "'Giobbe il giusto, degradato ad animale da esperimento': Maurizio Cohen's La gabbia" in F. Orsitto, ed., *L'Altro e l'Altrove nella cultura italiana* (Cuneo: Nerosubianco, 2011). "Io sono un centauro: Betrayal in Primo Levi's Quaestio de Centauris" in *NEMLA Italian Studies* 32 (2010).

DANIELE FIORETTI (Ph.D. University of Wisconsin, Madison; Ph.D. Università degli Studi di Firenze) is Lecturer of Italian at Miami University (Ohio). He is mainly interested in Italian modern and contemporary literature, cinema and culture. He published articles on Pier Paolo Pasolini, Paolo Volponi, Alessandro Blasetti, Roberto Minervini, and others. Among his publications: Paolo Volponi, *Scrivo a te come guardandomi allo specchio. Lettere a Pasolini 1954-1975* (Florence: Polistampa, 2009); *Carte di fabbrica. La narrativa industriale in Italia 1934-1989* (Pescara: Tracce, 2013) and *Utopia and Dystopia in Postwar Italian Literature – Pasolini, Calvino, Sanguineti, Volponi* (Palgrave Macmillan, 2017).

ROBERT HACKETT (Ph.D. Università di Bologna) is a freelance translator of French and Italian into English. Between 2012 and 2017 he edited and translated for Slow Food, Context-US and Edizioni BD srl. He has also taught at Indiana University, The International School in Olbia, and at the Sant'Anna Institute in Sorrento. Among his publications: "The Voices of 'Women' in Medieval Italian Poetry: Compiuta Donzella and Guittone d'Arezzo" in M. Marino & G. Spani, eds., *Donne del Mediterraneo, Rappresentazioni e autorappresentazioni* (Lanciano: Carabba 2017); "The Bible in Medieval Love Lyrics: A Fundamental Element of European Poetry Books" in A. Molinari & M. Dallapiazza, eds., *Mittelalterphilologien heute. Eine Standortbestimmung. Teil 1: Die germanischen Philologien*, Würzburg:

Königshausen u. Neumann, 2015; "Freedom of Heart, Freedom of Sentiment," in R. Campagnoli, *Mondi diversi* (Bologna: Clueb, 2011).

GIOVANNI SPANI (Ph.D. Indiana University) is Associate Professor of Italian at the College of the Holy Cross. He taught at Indiana University, Trinity College, Middlebury College and Bowdoin College. Among his publications: *La cronachistica toscana del Trecento: trascrivere, compilare e compendiare la storia* (Alessandria: Edizioni Dell'Orso, 2014); *Visioni Mediterranee: Itinerari e Migrazioni Culturali* (edited with Marco Marino) (Lanciano: Carabba, 2016); *Donne del Mediterraneo. Saggi interdisciplinari* (edited with Marco Marino) Firenze: Società Editrice Fiorentina, 2017; *Donne del Mediterraneo. Rappresentazioni e autorappresentazioni* (edited with Marco Marino) (Lanciano: Carabba, 2017); "A Case of Sudden-Death in *Decameron* IV.6: Aortic Dissection or Atrial Mixoma?." *Circulation Research. Journal of the American Heart Association* 119 (2016); "Giovanni Boccaccio's (1313 – 1375) Disease and Demise: The Final Untold Tale of Liver and Heart Failure." *Homo. Journal of Comparative Human Biology* 68.4 (2017).

SAGGISTICA

Taking its name from the Italian—which means essays, essay writing, or non-fiction—*Saggisitca* is a refereed book series dedicated to the study of all topics and cultural productions that fall under what we might consider that larger umbrella of all things Italian and Italian/ American.

Vito Zagarrio
  The "Un-Happy Ending": Re-viewing The Cinema of Frank Capra.
  2011. ISBN 978-1-59954-005-4. Volume 1.
Paolo A. Giordano, Editor
  The Hyphenate Writer and The Legacy of Exile. 2010. ISBN 978-1-
  59954-007-8. Volume 2.
Dennis Barone
  America / Trattabili. 2011. ISBN 978-1-59954-018-4. Volume 3.
Fred L. Gardaphè
  The Art of Reading Italian Americana. 2011. ISBN 978-1-59954-019-1.
  Volume 4.
Anthony Julian Tamburri
  Re-viewing Italian Americana: Generalities and Specificities on Cinema.
  2011. ISBN 978-1-59954-020-7. Volume 5.
Sheryl Lynn Postman
  *An Italian Writer's Journey through American Realities: Giose
  Rimanelli's English Novels. "The most tormented decade of America:
  the 60s"* ISBN 978-1-59954-034-4. Volume 6.
Luigi Fontanella
  Migrating Words: Italian Writers in the United States. 2012. ISBN
  978-1-59954-041-2. Volume 7.
Peter Covino & Dennis Barone, Editors
  Essays on Italian American Literature and Culture. 2012. ISBN 978-1-
  59954-035-1. Volume 8.
Gianfranco Viesti
  Italy at the Crossroads. 2012. ISBN 978-1-59954-071-9. Volume 9.
Peter Carravetta, Editor
  *Discourse Boundary Creation (LOGOS TOPOS POIESIS): A
  Festschrift in Honor of Paolo Valesio.* ISBN 978-1-59954-036-8.
  Volume 10.

Antonio Vitti and Anthony Julian Tamburri, Editors
  Europe, Italy, and the Mediterranean. ISBN 978-1-59954-073-3. Volume 11.
Vincenzo Scotti
  Pax Mafiosa or War: Twenty Years after the Palermo Massacres. 2012. ISBN 978-1-59954-074-0. Volume 12.
Anthony Julian Tamburri, Editor
  Meditations on Identity. Meditazioni su identità. ISBN 978-1-59954-082-5. Volume 13.
Peter Carravetta, Editor
  Theater of the Mind, Stage of History. A Festschrift in Honor of Mario Mignone. ISBN 978-1-59954-083-2. Volume 14.
Lorenzo Del Boca
  Italy's Lies. Debunking History's Lies So That Italy Might Become A "Normal Country". ISBN 978-1-59954-084-9. Volume 15.
George Guida
  Spectacles of Themselves. Essays in Italian American Popular Culture and Literature. ISBN 978-1-59954-090-0. Volume 16.
Antonio Vitti and Anthony Julian Tamburri, Editors
  Mare Nostrum: prospettive di un dialogo tra alterità e mediterraneità. ISBN 978-1-59954-100-6. Volume 17.
Patrizia Salvetti
  Rope and Soap. Lynchings of Italians in the United States. ISBN 978-1-59954-101-3. Volume 18.
Sheryl Lynn Postman and Anthony Julian Tamburri, Editors
  Re-reading Rimanelli in America: Six Decades in the United States. ISBN 978-1-59954-102-0. Volume 19.
Pasquale Verdicchio
  Bound by Distance. Rethinking Nationalism Through the Italian Diaspora. ISBN 978-1-59954-103-7. Volume 20.
Peter Carravetta
  After Identity. Migration, Critique, Italian American Culture. ISBN 978-1-59954-072-6. Volume 21.
Antonio Vitti and Anthony Julian Tamburri, Editors
  The Mediterranean As Seen by Insiders and Outsiders. ISBN 978-1-59954-107-5. Volume 22.
Eugenio Ragni
  Giose 1959. Un "Suicidio" Annunciato. American Culture. ISBN 978-1-59954-109-9. Volume 23.

SAGGISTICA

Taking its name from the Italian—which means essays, essay writing, or non-fiction—*Saggisitca* is a refereed book series dedicated to the study of all topics and cultural productions that fall under what we might consider that larger umbrella of all things Italian and Italian/American.

Vito Zagarrio
   The "Un-Happy Ending": Re-viewing The Cinema of Frank Capra. 2011. ISBN 978-1-59954-005-4. Volume 1.
Paolo A. Giordano, Editor
   The Hyphenate Writer and The Legacy of Exile. 2010. ISBN 978-1-59954-007-8. Volume 2.
Dennis Barone
   America / Trattabili. 2011. ISBN 978-1-59954-018-4. Volume 3.
Fred L. Gardaphè
   The Art of Reading Italian Americana. 2011. ISBN 978-1-59954-019-1. Volume 4.
Anthony Julian Tamburri
   Re-viewing Italian Americana: Generalities and Specificities on Cinema. 2011. ISBN 978-1-59954-020-7. Volume 5.
Sheryl Lynn Postman
   An Italian Writer's Journey through American Realities: Giose Rimanelli's English Novels. "The most tormented decade of America: the 60s" ISBN 978-1-59954-034-4. Volume 6.
Luigi Fontanella
   Migrating Words: Italian Writers in the United States. 2012. ISBN 978-1-59954-041-2. Volume 7.
Peter Covino & Dennis Barone, Editors
   Essays on Italian American Literature and Culture. 2012. ISBN 978-1-59954-035-1. Volume 8.
Gianfranco Viesti
   Italy at the Crossroads. 2012. ISBN 978-1-59954-071-9. Volume 9.
Peter Carravetta, Editor
   Discourse Boundary Creation (LOGOS TOPOS POIESIS): A Festschrift in Honor of Paolo Valesio. ISBN 978-1-59954-036-8. Volume 10.

Antonio Vitti and Anthony Julian Tamburri, Editors
Europe, Italy, and the Mediterranean. ISBN 978-1-59954-073-3. Volume 11.

Vincenzo Scotti
Pax Mafiosa or War: Twenty Years after the Palermo Massacres. 2012. ISBN 978-1-59954-074-0. Volume 12.

Anthony Julian Tamburri, Editor
Meditations on Identity. Meditazioni su identità. ISBN 978-1-59954-082-5. Volume 13.

Peter Carravetta, Editor
Theater of the Mind, Stage of History. A Festschrift in Honor of Mario Mignone. ISBN 978-1-59954-083-2. Volume 14.

Lorenzo Del Boca
Italy's Lies. Debunking History's Lies So That Italy Might Become A "Normal Country". ISBN 978-1-59954-084-9. Volume 15.

George Guida
Spectacles of Themselves. Essays in Italian American Popular Culture and Literature. ISBN 978-1-59954-090-0. Volume 16.

Antonio Vitti and Anthony Julian Tamburri, Editors
Mare Nostrum: prospettive di un dialogo tra alterità e mediterraneità. ISBN 978-1-59954-100-6. Volume 17.

Patrizia Salvetti
Rope and Soap. Lynchings of Italians in the United States. ISBN 978-1-59954-101-3. Volume 18.

Sheryl Lynn Postman and Anthony Julian Tamburri, Editors
Re-reading Rimanelli in America: Six Decades in the United States. ISBN 978-1-59954-102-0. Volume 19.

Pasquale Verdicchio
Bound by Distance. Rethinking Nationalism Through the Italian Diaspora. ISBN 978-1-59954-103-7. Volume 20.

Peter Carravetta
After Identity. Migration, Critique, Italian American Culture. ISBN 978-1-59954-072-6. Volume 21.

Antonio Vitti and Anthony Julian Tamburri, Editors
The Mediterranean As Seen by Insiders and Outsiders. ISBN 978-1-59954-107-5. Volume 22.

Eugenio Ragni
Giose 1959. Un "Suicidio" Annunciato. American Culture. ISBN 978-1-59954-109-9. Volume 23.

www.ingramcontent.com/pod-product-compliance
Lightning Source LLC
Chambersburg PA
CBHW020156090426
42734CB00008B/839